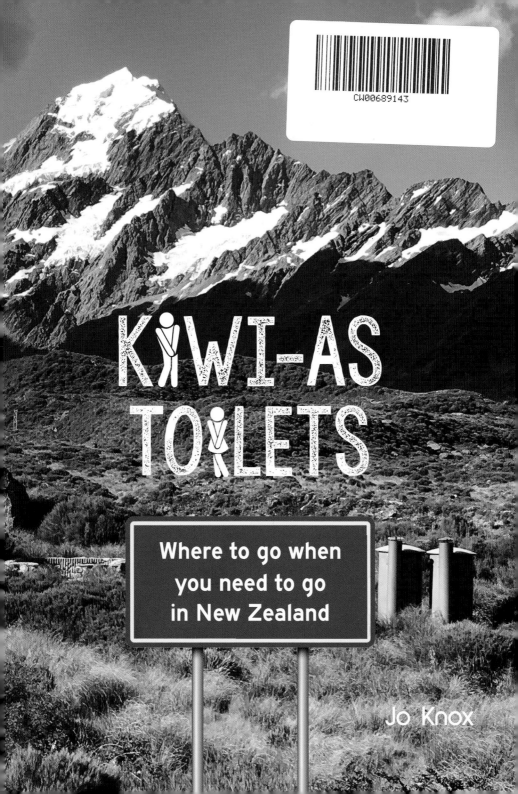

KIWI-AS TOILETS

Where to go when you need to go in New Zealand

Jo Knox

ACKNOWLEDGMENTS

'It takes a village to raise a child,' they say, and I feel something similar applies to the creation and completion of this book. From the conception of the idea through to publishing the finishing product, there have been so many individuals who have contributed, helped, advised and supported me in some way. Researching New

Zealand's top toilets would not have been possible without the assistance from many council personnel and individuals at i-SITE visitor information centres who sourced information for me and provided me with relevant contacts. To the business owners and operators, and the designers, architects and artists involved in the toilets that feature in this book, I thank you so much for the time and information you so generously gave to me. I hope that you see the rewards from this book you so very much deserve through the generation of even more interest in and appreciation of you and your work or business.

Thank you to my family, parents, brother and friends who have continued to ask how my work is coming along, given me encouragement and even found a few toilets for me to add to the collection. Your on-going interest and support really kept me going. In particular, I must acknowledge the support I have had from my long-suffering husband, Trev, who over the course of the year-and-a-half of research and writing, grew increasingly suspicious of any weekend away I might suggest. 'Are we going there just to look at more toilets?' he'd ask. To which I'd reply, 'Erm, maybe I'll check to see if there are any,' knowing full well that there were at least three I wanted to check out! I loved how you attempted to feign a complete lack of interest in my project but always kept your eyes out for top toilets for me while we were on the road. Thank you also for all those times you risked being seen as a complete weirdo by going into the men's toilets with a camera! To Oli and Toby, our two boys, thank you for your enthusiasm in my book and the parts you played in 'researching'. Memories of you exiting toilets commenting, 'Nah, not book-worthy', or, 'Just bog-standard ones, Mum!' will stay with me throughout my years!

TOILET
LOCATIONS

PREFACE

This compendium of conveniences was inspired by frequenting a number of loos for my number ones and twos during my New Zealand travels. After many journeys around New Zealand, I realised I was planning stops along some of my well-trodden routes to avoid dumping in dumps in favour of lovelier lavs. Some, I had spotted for being spotless, some were individually interesting, and other restrooms were remembered for their touch of humour, art or quirkiness. I began to wonder how many more fancy flushers I might be missing out on.

My research revealed that many of New Zealand's towns and businesses have joined a movement towards spotlighting places for our movements. It seems that Kiwis have been on a roll revamping revolting restrooms from somewhere you'd only go if you were desperate to places you want to go to when you don't even need to! In efforts to make the most of what is usually a hurried and unremarkable experience, tasteless toilets have been transformed into tourist attractions. I realised that while most travel guides might include best places to stay and eat, showcase the stunning scenery or promote a plethora of activities that the country has to offer, they avoided the dirty business of where to do your business! What was needed was a guide to New Zealand's terrific toilets.

Believing my idea stunk somewhat, my husband initially poo-pooed my idea of compiling a book of New Zealand's best bogs! However, nature was calling me; I was bursting to do this and determined to follow through with my plan. I had nothing to loos! And the quest to personally punish the porcelain of the most remarkable restrooms in New Zealand resulted in the road trip of a lifetime. Frequenting the funniest facilities, most decorative dunnies and best loos with views that New Zealand has to offer provided a reason for our family to travel and visit places that might otherwise have not featured on our 'must-do' list. It is my hope that this compilation encourages others to make similar emergency pit stop detours from the better-travelled routes that the majority of tourists find themselves following.

HUNDERTWASSER
TOILETS

INTRODUCTION

No other country does toilets like New Zealand does! And yet interesting toilets are possibly one of New Zealand's best-kept secrets! Ask someone what New Zealand is famous for, and toilets probably won't appear their list... yet... But they should! Kiwi-as toilets aims to start the ball rolling (or should that be ballcock rolling?!) in giving our  country's top toilets the recognition they deserve and inspiring others to join the movement.

This toilet guide provides a light-hearted overview of some of New Zealand's most interesting lavatories. While it is not a travel guide per-se in that it doesn't necessarily include information about accommodation, restaurants, transportation and activities, it provides a brief overview of the featuring toilets' locations. Alongside each toilet's photograph, a rundown of its best features is provided, enabling readers to learn about the toilet's history or story, and the designers, artists and community groups involved. The order of the 65 Kiwi-as toilets in the book represents a tourist toilet trail that can be taken in order to pay each one a visit that tracks (roughly) north to south as shown on the map provided (see page 3).

The toilet contents are separated (not at the sewerage treatment plant) into different categories. Most are public toilets, but others are marked as being 'business owned'. I found many toilets had a strong community connection, where local groups of people had collaborated and volunteered their time and services to create public facilities that the whole community could be proud of. These are marked under the heading 'Community'. Some toilets fall under the headings of 'Artistic', 'Architectural' or 'Wonderfully weird'. Of these, a few are 'Award-winning' for their art or architecture. Although the views cannot be enjoyed from the seat of the pan, a number of toilets are marked as 'Loos with views' because they are located in stunning scenery and the beautiful view is obvious as soon as you exit. Toilets identified as being 'Tops with families' are ones that are fun and humorous in their own right, or at destinations that are fabulous for families day tripping or holidaying, or in cafés and tourist attractions that families will enjoy. Finally, some toilets are listed under the 'Educational/Historic' heading for their location at historic sites or for providing sources of education. My intention is that these categories may help readers to better select which ones to 'tick off' their toilet bucket list when they travel around New Zealand – an empty check box is provided next to each one on the Toilet Contents pages for this purpose. But I'm secretly hoping that readers are inspired to grace each and every one of these toilet seats with their bare backsides!

It is not my intention to provide an exhaustive list of all the toilets in New Zealand or to necessarily provide a review of a toilet's functionality or cleanliness. There are free apps available these purposes, for example Toilet Finder or, the app I used, CamperMate. CamperMate links with Google Maps to enable users to locate and rate New Zealand's public toilets. I acknowledge that there may be other toilets worthy of accolades that didn't make my cut and I also hope there will be other flash facilities to come. I look forward to hearing about these – maybe I will add them in a second edition of the book – Kiwi-as Toilets: Volume Number Twos?!!

Following the guide will direct you where to go when you need to go and to toilets you'll want to visit even when you don't need to go. As you make your bladder gladder at these convenient convenience stops, you may be blown away by the history, the stories, the ingenuity, the creativity and the resourcefulness revealed behind each one, while enjoying New Zealand's attractions, destinations and scenery along the way. Taking a tiki tour of New Zealand's top toilet stops may provide additional places of interest to your trip and add a touch of quirkiness, humour and surprise to your photo collection and memories of New Zealand. And who knows, Kiwi khazis may even start to be considered Kiwiana; the cistern may become as celebrated and synonymous with New Zealand as rugby, L&P, sheep, kiwis and jandals. New Zealand knows how to do toilets. Toilets Kiwi style. These are 'Kiwi-as toilets'!

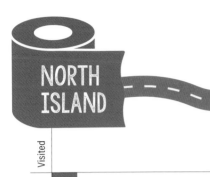

NORTH ISLAND

Visited			Page	Business owned	Community	Artistic	Architectural	Award winning	Wonderfully weird	Loos with views	Tops for families	Educational/Historic
	1	Hundertwasser Public Toilets, Kawakawa	14		🚽	🚽	🚽		🚽		🚽	
	2	Maiki Hill Public Toilets, Paihia	18		🚽	🚽			🚽	🚽	🚽	
	3	Waitangi Treaty Ground Toilets, Waitangi	20					🚽	🚽			🚽	🚽
	4	Waipu Cove Public Toilets, Waipu	22		🚽			🚽		🚽	🚽	🚽
	5	Camp Waipu Cove, Waipu	24	🚽		🚽					🚽	
	6	McLeod's Pizza Barn and Taphouse, Waipu	25	🚽					🚽		🚽	
	7	Matakana Public Toilets, Matakana	28		🚽	🚽	🚽				🚽	
	8	Sullivan's Bay DOC Campground Toilets, Mahurangi West	30				🚽			🚽	🚽	
	9	Western Reserve Public Toilets, Orewa	32				🚽			🚽	🚽	
	10	Stanmore Bay Park and Reserve Public Toilets, Hibiscus Coast	34		🚽	🚽	🚽			🚽	🚽	
	11	Kaipara Coast Plant Centre and Sculpture Gardens, Kaukapakapa	36	🚽			🚽				🚽	
	12	Creek Lane Public Toilets, Helensville	38				🚽		🚽			
	13	Maungauika/North Head Public Toilets, Devonport	40							🚽	🚽	🚽
	14	White + Wong's, Auckland	42	🚽					🚽			
	15	Grafton Bridge Public Toilets and Shelter, Auckland	44					🚽				🚽
	16	Hot Water Beach Public Toilets, Hot Water Beach	46					🚽		🚽	🚽	
	17	Hahei Holiday Resort, Hahei	48	🚽					🚽		🚽	
	18	Waihi Beach Public Toilets, Waihi Beach	50			🚽						
	19	Waihi Beach Surf Club Toilets, Waihi Beach	52					🚽	🚽		🚽	🚽
	20	Diggelmann Park Public Toilets, Katikati	54					🚽				🚽

Visited			Page	Business owned	Community	Artistic	Architectural	Award winning	Wonderfully weird	Loos with views	Tops for families	Educational/Historic
	21	Sheepdog Public Toilets, Tirau	56		🚽				🚽		🚽	
	22	Outhouse Public Toilets, Tirau	58		🚽				🚽		🚽	
	23	The Redwoods Shroud Art Toilets, Rotorua	60		🚽	🚽	🚽			🚽	🚽	
	24	Waipa Valley Bike Park Public Toilets, Rotorua	64		🚽	🚽					🚽	
	25	Lake Tikitapu (Blue Lake) Public Toilets, Lake Tikitapu	66		🚽					🚽	🚽	
	26	Otorohanga Public Toilets, Otorohanga	68									
	27	Benneydale Public Toilets, Benneydale	70			🚽						
	28	Hipapatua/Reid's Farm Recreation Reserve, Taupo	72		🚽					🚽	🚽	
	29	Taupo Central Public Toilets, Taupo	74		🚽							
	30	Emporium Eatery and Bar, Napier	75	🚽								🚽
	31	Bay Skate, Napier	78	🚽		🚽					🚽	
	32	Clifton Road Reserve Public Toilets, Hastings	80				🚽	🚽	🚽			
	33	Jailhouse Public Toilets, Ongaonga	82									🚽
	34	Tongariro Alpine Crossing Toilets, Tongariro National Park	84							🚽		
	35	Waiouru Public Toilets, Waiouru	86				🚽	🚽				🚽
	36	Stratford Public Toilets, Stratford	88									🚽
	37	Eltham Public Toilets, Eltham	90			🚽	🚽					
	38	Tui HQ Café, Mangatainoka	92	🚽								🚽
	39	Kumutoto Public Toilets, Wellington	94			🚽	🚽	🚽	🚽		🚽	
	40	The Fork and Brewer, Wellington	96	🚽					🚽			

SOUTH ISLAND

Visited			Page	Business owned	Community	Artistic	Architectural	Award winning	Wonderfully weird	Loos with views	Tops for families	Educational/Historic
	41	Mussel Inn, Onekaka	100	🚽					🚽			
	42	Pohara Public Toilets, Pohara	102				🚽					
	43	Takaka Public Toilets, Takaka	103				🚽	🚽	🚽		🚽	
	44	Jester House Café, Motueka	104	🚽			🚽			🚽	🚽	
	45	Kaikoura Town Centre Public Toilets, Kaikoura	106		🚽	🚽						
	46	South End Public Toilets, Kaikoura	108						🚽		🚽	🚽
	47	Margaret Mahy Playground, Christchurch	110		🚽	🚽						🚽
	48	Dux Central, Christchurch	112	🚽					🚽			
	49	Wunderbar, Lyttelton	115	🚽					🚽			
	50	HarBar Beach Café and Bar, Akaroa	118	🚽						🚽		
	51	Mt Hutt Ski Area, Canterbury	120	🚽				🚽		🚽	🚽	
	52	Friendly Bay Playground Toilets, Oamaru	122								🚽	
	53	Hooker Valley Track DOC Toilets, Aoraki/Mt Cook	126							🚽		

Visited		Page	Business owned	Community	Artistic	Architectural	Award winning	Wonderfully weird	Loos with views	Tops for families	Educational/Historic
54	Puzzling World, Wanaka	128	🚽	🚽				🚽		🚽	🚽
55	Cromwell Town Centre Public Toilet & Bus Shelter, Cromwell	130				🚽	🚽				
56	Cromwell Heritage Precinct Public Toilet, Cromwell	132				🚽			🚽	🚽	🚽
57	Pub on a Wharf, Queenstown	134	🚽								
57	Muskets and Moonshine, Queenstown	134	🚽					🚽			
57	Jervois Steak House, Queenstown	134	🚽					🚽			
57	Cowboys, Queenstown	134	🚽					🚽			
58	Oast House, Creeksyde Holiday Park, Queenstown	138	🚽	🚽				🚽		🚽	
59	Roxburgh Public Toilets, Roxburgh	140			🚽						🚽
60	North Mavora Lake DOC Toilet, Mavora	142							🚽	🚽	
61	Bill Richardson Transport World and Classic Motorcycle Mecca, Invercargill	144	🚽					🚽		🚽	🚽
62	Dig This Invercargill, Invercargill	148	🚽					🚽		🚽	

NORTH ISLAND

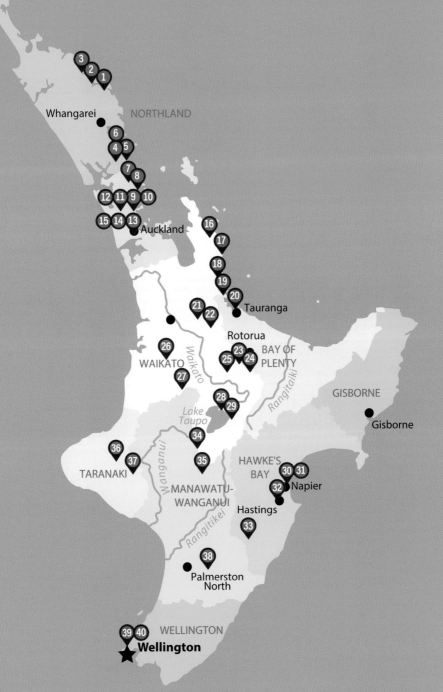

NORTHLAND

Whangarei

Auckland

BAY OF
PLENTY

Rotorua

Tauranga

WAIKATO

GISBORNE

Gisborne

Lake
Taupo

HAWKE'S
BAY

TARANAKI

Napier

MANAWATU-
WANGANUI

Hastings

Palmerston
North

WELLINGTON

Wellington

Waikato

Rangitaiki

Wanganui

Rangitikei

HUNDERTWASSER PUBLIC TOILETS
39–43 Gillies St, Kawakawa, Northland 0210

NZ's most famous and photographed fancy flushers!

Unquestionably, these truly unique toilets have put Kawakawa on the New Zealand tourist trail since their creation in 1999, attracting visitors from all around the world. Driving through this small town, the colourful sculptures, mosaics, copper and cobblestones of the town's public toilets are unmissable. These facilities weren't cheap, costing $130,000, but they certainly sparked the toilet transformation movement in New Zealand, and inspired other towns to

follow suit in changing the humble water closet into focal-point flushers.

Friedensreich Hundertwasser, one Austria's foremost artists and architects of the twentieth century, moved to the Northland town in the mid-1970s. Hundertwasser designed and gifted the toilets to the town he loved, and the local community mirrored his generosity by volunteering services to the construction process. Built around a living tree that grows up through the ceiling into a rooftop garden, these toilets are constructed mostly with recycled materials, reflecting Hundertwasser's environmentally considerate approach to architecture. Bricks recycled from the recently demolished Bank of New Zealand, colourful tiles of different shapes and sizes, empty bottles, steel, copper and bits and pieces from his own studio were all used to create what was to be Hundertwasser's final work of art and the only Hundertwasser structure in the southern hemisphere.

The fully functional toilet block serves as a memorial to Friedensreich Hundertwasser and has received attention on a scale that Hundertwasser himself could never have anticipated. International television documentaries have featured the facility and tourists visit daily in their busloads. And while there's something decidedly unnerving about having crowds of photo-happy tourists waving cameras around as you attempt to perform what is the most basic human function, it's virtually impossible to resist the urge to join in and record your own personal potty experience!

Hundertwasser designed and gifted the toilets to the town he loved, and the local community mirrored his generosity by volunteering services to the construction process

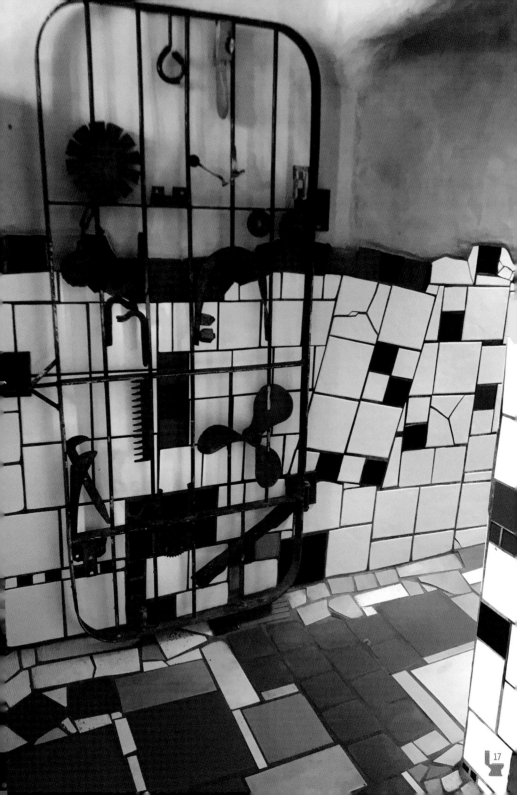

17

MAIKI HILL PUBLIC TOILETS
69 Marsden Rd, Paihia 0247

From eyesore to eye-catching, 'Paihia's Wee Toilets' are a funky piece of artwork.

Paihia is a bustling seaside town in the heart of the Bay of Islands. Take a walk along Paihia's waterfront and enjoy the vista from bars and cafés on the boardwalk with its coloured lights, fountains, sculptures, giant board game and large illuminated map. There is even a free library in an old phone booth, and a public piano is wheeled out daily for anyone to tinkle the ivories on. From the wharf, a variety of trips are offered out into the bay by cruise boat or yacht. The small historic town of Russell is an easy 15-minute passenger ferry ride across the bay from Paihia. There you can savour the relaxed atmosphere, strolling around some of the oldest buildings in New Zealand or sipping a cold glass of beer while watching the sunset from the balcony of the Duke of Marlborough, New Zealand's oldest licenced pub.

There is even a free library in an old phone booth, and a public piano is wheeled out daily for anyone to tinkle the ivories on.

Paihia's primo potties are found at the base of Maiki Hill, which is located on the waterfront of central Paihia. This once grotty and unappealing ablution block had a reputation of being one of New Zealand's worst toilet facilities until being transformed in 2012. Embarrassed by what was the town's eyesore, Focus Paihia and their Paihia Phantom Placemaker Projects drove a community enterprise involving a team of local tradies and businesses that volunteered their time to magically transform the toilet block within just ten days and with a budget of just $15,000. The toilet block, designed by David Engwicht from Creative Communities International, has a quirky Flintstone-like look with its roughly shaped open entrance and walls, which are formed with exposed aggregate concrete. You cannot help but smile upon seeing the stainless steel toilet pans utilised as plant pots both inside the block and on the rooftop garden, and the individual pottery letters above the entrance proudly spelling 'Paihia's Wee Toilet'.

WAITANGI TREATY GROUNDS TOILETS

Te Kōngahu Museum of Waitangi, 1 Tau Henare Drive, Waitangi, Bay of Islands 0293

A hut in the bush.

A visit to the Waitangi Treaty Grounds, New Zealand's most important historic site, and Te Kōngahu Museum of Waitangi allows you to step back in time and appreciate the nation's birthplace. The waterfront location of the grounds allows for stunning views over the Bay of Islands. The impressive architecture of the buildings within the grounds cleverly blends Māori cultural influences with large, modern structures, and the toilet block, or Whare Horoi, is no exception. Resembling a large hut in native bush, the building makes use of beautiful natural timber that complements the surrounding mānuka trees. However, as you enter, the large glass walls, concreted and tiled solid surfaces, and impressive fixtures and fittings create a delightfully modern contrast to the natural

> ...cleverly blends Māori cultural influences with large, modern structures

aspects. Skylight windows along a large gabled roof and a floor-to-ceiling glass wall at the end of the room flood the interior with natural light and connect it with its natural bush surroundings. HB Architecture was responsible for the award-winning concept, which was built in 2009, receiving a New Zealand Institute of Architects award in 2010 in the Small Project category.

WAIPU COVE PUBLIC TOILETS, WAIPU

901 Cove Rd, Waipu 0582

Why poo at Waipu?
Well you can learn a thing or two!

It would be a crying shame if there were no book-worthy toilets at a town with this name, now, wouldn't it? Fear not. Waipu and its surrounds does not disappoint!

Waipu's strong Scottish heritage is apparent as soon as you cross into the town's border, with a sign that welcomes you a hundred thousand times in Gaelic: Ceud mile failte. Continuing into Waipu, you encounter many Scottish-sounding roads – The Braigh, Argyle Street, Braemar Lane and Lochalsh Drive. The real Scottish celebrations, however, occur on New Year's Day with Waipu's famous Highland Games, and again later in July during Tartan Week.

If you're wondering where the connection with Scotland originated from, allow Waipu Cove's public toilets to tell the tale. A series of murals wrap around the entire beachside toilet block depicting the story of Scottish immigration to New Zealand, via Nova Scotia, in 1851. The mural includes the Waipu anniversary tartan, depictions of camping at Waipu Cove in the 1930s and a portrait of the settlement leader, Reverend Norman McLeod. The work by artist Daniel Mills was researched with assistance from the local community, local iwi, the Waipu Cove Reserve Board and the Waipu Museum. Taking out the professional category of a Resene Mural Masterpiece competition in 2007, Daniel's work attracts a lot of attention and has even been used as a resource for history lessons with school groups.

A series of murals wrap around the entire beachside toilet block depicting the story of Scottish immigration to New Zealand, via Nova Scotia, in 1851.

CAMP WAIPU COVE
869 Cove Rd, Waipu 0582

Waipu some more?
Well, these toilets are worth it!

Following on from the success of his work at the Waipu Cove public toilets, in 2016 Daniel Mills was commissioned to decorate three toilet blocks in Camp Waipu Cove. Situated alongside the unspoilt beach, the campground has been a family holiday haven for many generations. Each toilet block in the camp has a unique, locally influenced design. The first celebrates the work of the surf life-savers and the popularity of surfing in Waipu. The second block is adorned with a larger-than-life display of the marine life to be found in the local Bream Bay waters. And if you're wondering how to best spend your time in Waipu, the third block, found in the northern part of the campground, showcases the best things to see and do in Waipu. The high quality of these stunning pieces of art reflects the 200-plus hours that Daniel dedicated to each of these murals.

MCLEOD'S PIZZA BARN AND TAPHOUSE
2 Cove Rd, Waipu 0510

'Yer aff yer heid' if you miss these lads'
and lasses' loos. Och aye!

Fill up on tasty, traditional pub food or pizza at McLeod's Pizza Barn and Taphouse, which is located in Waipu's former post office. Tapping into the heritage of Reverend Norman McLeod and the early Highland settlers, this quirky eatery is draped in tartan and is so Scottish that all that is missing is a tartan-kilt-wearing Highland bull... Correction. It actually does have one!!

The Barn, originally renowned for its creative and topping-loaded pizzas, has become just as famous for its brewery.

The Barn, originally renowned for its creative and topping-loaded pizzas, has become just as famous for its brewery. After you've partaken in sampling a few of their finest craft beers, a trip to the 'Lads' and 'Lasses' toilets, adorned with 1950s memorabilia, may be necessary! Lasses can check out 1950s fashion from the cheesy catalogue pages-cum-wallpaper in their restrooms. With everything bar the crocheted dolly loo roll cover, the furnishings look like they've come straight from Nana's house. The Lads' loos are a sporty and musical trip down memory lane, decorated with LP covers of Kiwi classics and photographs of local sports teams from years gone by.

MATAKANA PUBLIC TOILETS
Matakana Road, Warkworth 0985

Toilets that prove that sometimes more than a penny needs spending in order to spend a penny!

Just an hour's drive north of Auckland, Matakana Village feels a million miles away from the hustle and bustle of the city. The vibrant riverside village is home to independent specialised shopping, arts and crafts, galleries, cafés, restaurants and a stunning arthouse cinema complex. There are award-winning wines to be tasted at wineries along the Matakana wine trail, and the Matakana Farmers' Market every Saturday morning offers produce from local artisans, growers and farmers.

Sitting majestically between the banks of the Matakana River and the Matakana roundabout, this iconic toilet block is one of the country's most artistic. The toilets showcase a design created by local Steffan de Haan, a first-year Fine Arts student at Auckland University, who entered and won Matakana's public toilet design competition. The elegant curved shape of the pair of toilet buildings resembles the hulls of salvaged ships, and the buildings feature recycled kauri wood – a symbolic reference to the history of boat building in the area. Stained glass 'porthole' windows add to the nautical feel. Statuesque sentinels' half-faces formed from moulded concrete guard the toilet entrances.

The toilets were a source of controversy for some time, with strong opposition leading to a change of location, lengthy delays and additional expense. However, the sense of community shone through with one-third of the cost being generated from fundraising, and many artists and contractors donating their time. Taking seven years to complete, the toilets officially opened to the public in 2009. At almost three times the cost of the average convenience block, these toilets cost around $400,000 to build and have been insured for $500,000, proving that sometimes more than a penny needs spending in order to spend a penny!

Statuesque sentinels
half-faces formed
from moulded concrete
guard the toilet
entrance

SULLIVAN'S BAY DOC CAMPGROUND TOILETS

Mahurangi Regional Park, 192 Ngarewa Drive, Mahurangi West, Warkworth 0983

Shipshape for your floaters!

The Sullivan's Bay Campground is set in the picturesque Mahurangi Regional Park and is a popular location for camping, swimming or picnicking. The views across the bay seen when driving over the ridge before descending into the campground are simply stunning, and the water is often teaming with sailing boats. With no development surrounding the bay, you can enjoy the simplicity of camping right next to the beach and sea while being protected by hills on the other side.

Six bright and airy unisex toilet stalls were installed here in 2016, thankfully replacing the existing basic, long drop toilets. The red and green colours of this block mimic the surrounding tree-clad site, especially when the bright red pohutukawa and rata tree flowers are in bloom. Laser-cut screens of corten steel above the toilets provide light and ventilation. These screens also act as a bird

Mahurangi Regional Park

This natural masterpiece is cared for by the Auckland Regional Council

restriction device and are fittingly decorated with silhouettes of native birds which are all found in the park. Another, larger, screen in front of the toilets is provided with safety in mind to restrict young children from running directly out of any cubicle into the paths of vehicles driving or parking nearby. The nautical design depicted on these screens is of a cutter built around the 1870s by John Darrach and serves as a reminder of the historical ship building that took place across the water at Lagoon Bay in Mahurangi East.

WESTERN RESERVE PUBLIC TOILETS

214 Hibiscus Coast Hwy, Orewa 0931

Toilets worth stopping at to smell the roses (well, hibiscus flowers)!

Just 20 minutes north of Auckland, Orewa's magnificent 3-km long beach is the perfect destination for relaxing walks, safe swimming and family fun. At the southern end of this beautiful beach, the 7.5-km Te Ara Tahuna Estuary circuit track is popular for walking and cycling. The track runs past a popular skate park and traverses bush trails and quiet residential and park areas. Finish off your walk around the estuary with a visit to the Estuary Arts Centre. Entry into the gallery is free and it has a varied exhibition that showcases a wide variety of quality artwork.

The toilet block outside of the Estuary Arts Centre and overlooking the Te Ara Tahuna Estuary was upgraded in 2016. The Estuary Arts Centre Trust commissioned artist Ruby Watson to add a sculptural piece to the toilets. Taking inspiration from the birdlife in the area, Ruby created a series of metal sculpted birds taking flight from the rear wall and off the building. These modern facilities also feature two large tiled hibiscus flowers (mosaicked by artist Joy Bell) set into the concrete walls, a nod to their location on the Hibiscus Coast. The block conveniently includes changing rooms, a bicycle stand and a shaded seating area.

The Estuary Arts Centre Trust commissioned artist
Ruby Watson to add a sculptural piece to the toilets.

STANMORE BAY PARK & RESERVE PUBLIC TOILETS
Brightside Road, Hibiscus Coast 0932

The way these toilet blocks reflect their environment answers nature's call perfectly!

Stanmore Bay Park and Reserve is located next to the beach on the Hibiscus Coast. A strikingly colourful mural turned the Stanmore Bay Park facilities into tasteful toilets in 2013. Guided by local artist Anna Evans, children aged between 8 and 18 years painted the piece of artwork that had been created by digitally cutting and recomposing the students' own art. Working during weekends and school holidays, the team spent 120 hours completing the project. The New Zealand flora and fauna and sea vista mural is well suited to the beachside location of this boat-shaped toilet block.

> Guided by local artist Anna Evans, children aged between 8 and 18 years painted the piece of artwork...

KAIPARA COAST PLANT CENTRE & SCULPTURE GARDENS

1481 Kaipara Coast Highway, Kaukapakapa 0843

Spending a penny isn't always costly!

Set in a serene garden oasis, the Kaipara Coast Sculpture Gardens is a plant centre, a sculpture trail and a coffee stop. The sculpture trail is a gentle 1-km walk through beautiful gardens and native bush that twists and turns to intermittently reveal an eclectic collection of works sculpted from an array of materials. The creativity must have rubbed off onto owner David Bayly, who upgraded the gardens' toilets by upcycling watering cans into faucets and refashioning garden pails into basins.

The sculpture trail is a gentle 1-km walk through beautiful gardens and native bush

CREEK LANE PUBLIC TOILETS
1 Creek Lane, Helensville, Auckland 0800

Nice toilets, but no tanks!

Looking to put their toilets on the tourist map, Helensville put the tourist map on their toilets! The Helensville Riverside Heritage Group wanted to enhance the Kaipara riverside walkway and replace the existing toilets that had reached their use-by date with something that celebrated the area. Helensville local artist Jeff Thomson was commissioned to design the new-look loos that feature steel screen printed maps created from enlarged sections of Lands and Survey maps of the Kaipara Harbour and Helensville surrounds. Against the greens and blues of these wall panels, a steel grill under the roof featuring local marine life stands out. For this part, Jeff sought the help of a local skipper, who identified species that he'd come across in his 30 years of fishing on the Kaipara in a book of New Zealand marine life.

Helensville local artist Jeff Thomson was commissioned to design the new-look loos that feature steel screen printed maps...

Sitting at the entrance to the Kaipara riverside walkway on Creek Lane, the well-maintained, artistic toilets add to the heritage charm of the town. But while this part of the story remains a success, the grand vision for the water tank unfortunately sunk! With a goal of sustainability, the plan was for rainwater, collected from the adjacent shop roof and the toilet building's custom-made roof, to be used for flushing the toilets. Having previously created a water tank piece for Sculpture on the Gulf on Waiheke, Jeff was asked to create something similar for this 2010 project. Portholes in the tank provided viewing holes for displays housed inside the tank. Jeff's 3D images of marine life and historic shipwrecks, claimed by the treacherous Kaipara Harbour and Kaipara Bar, originally featured inside, with plans for this to be an ever-changing art exhibition. However, this part of the plan proved to be over-ambitious. The water collected was insufficient to effectively flush the toilets, and maintaining the clear water quality required to see the art was impracticable. It's hard to appreciate art through slimy, green water! Although it was 'tanks, but no tanks' to the sustainability and art exhibition dreams, the tank remains in place as a reminder of those 'best-laid plans'.

13

MAUNGAUIKA/NORTH HEAD PUBLIC TOILETS
Hauraki Gulf Maritime Park, Devonport, Auckland 0624

Fire away on this toilet with an explosive past!

Maungauika/North Head is located in Devonport, one of Auckland's prettiest and most historically authentic villages. North Head is one of the oldest of Auckland's 48 volcanic cones, and visitors can enjoy spectacular, panoramic views over the Hauraki Gulf and the city centre from the summit. In addition to being a beautiful place to visit, the reserve here is considered to be the most significant historical coastal defence site in New Zealand. The site holds a military tunnel complex and gun emplacements and fortifications, including an 8 inch disappearing gun built in 1886. Information can be found on many boards along the series of loop walking tracks, and a visual film history of North Head is shown at the old stone kitchen, built in 1885.

Next to this handsome stone building is the reserve's only toilet block. Although it isn't the prettiest, the toilet block and the land it stands on have a good story. The wooden toilet block was built in the 1970s using the shape of the fort's WWII searchlight emplacements as a design model. It was located on the site of a laboratory building from the old fort which was used for testing explosives and filling shells. This building had also been of wooden construction so that, in the event of an explosion, the debris would be light and the blast would be directed upwards. In an ironic twist of fate, while a blast never happened during its use as an explosive lab, when the building was subsequently used as a scout den, it burned down! It is amusingly appropriate that a site with such an explosive history continues to serve as place for explosions ... albeit of the personal kind!

Although it isn't the prettiest,
the toilet block and the land it
stands on have a good story

14

WHITE + WONG'S

149 Quay Street, Viaduct Harbour, Auckland 1010

The last thing you'd expect to find in a toilet is your destiny!

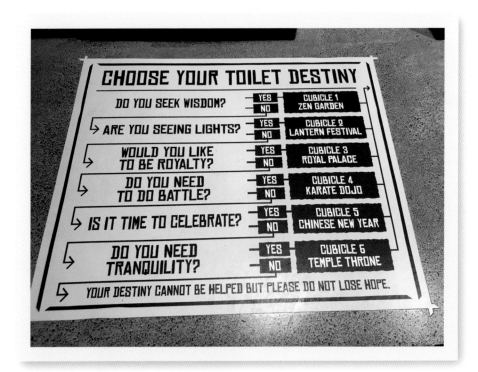

Located in the heart of Auckland's CBD, Auckland's vibrant Viaduct Harbour is lined with popular bars and restaurants overlooking the water, which is teaming with boats and superyachts. Here, White + Wong's offers a fusion of South East Asian cuisine from their harbourside restaurant. An 'East meets West' feel is achieved inside with colourful styling that incorporates Asian street and market influences, and guests can dine in the main dining area or in private dining dens.

A sign on the floor allows you to 'choose your toilet destiny',

The Far East has a long history of utilising a variety of divination techniques, but the fortune-telling method available to guests here is certainly not steeped in such tradition. Instead of visiting an oracle, you'll need to visit the toilet! A unisex restroom area transports you to a jungle-themed tiger enclosure where you are presented with a choice of six differently themed cubicles. A sign on the floor allows you to 'choose your toilet destiny', and, by answering a series of yes–no questions, you will 'go' in a zen garden, lantern festival, royal palace, karate dojo, Chinese New Year or temple throne-styled cubicle. Quite a novel take on the fortune cookie! Of course, your other option is to do what you'd do anywhere else and just wait for the first one that's vacant!

15

GRAFTON BRIDGE PUBLIC TOILETS & SHELTER

120 Symonds Street, Grafton, Auckland 1010

The most frequented flusher in New Zealand?

When Grafton Bridge was first built in 1910, it was put in the national and international spotlight for being the world's largest single-span, reinforced concrete bridge of its time. To coincide with the opening of Grafton Bridge, the public toilet block sitting adjacent to the bridge, on Symonds Street, was also opened, and so it too deserves its place in New Zealand's history books. It is thought to be the city's first women's public convenience block and the only building built for the dual purpose of sanitation and an electric tram shelter. However, your rear may get more than a little numb waiting for any public transport here – trams were decommissioned in 1928, and although the building was subsequently used as a bus stop and shelter, these too no longer stop here.

The building's symmetry and front façade design, embossed with the 1910 date of construction, is typical of the period's Edwardian Baroque architecture. However, the colourful woodland mural painted on the internal wall of the arch was painted much more recently. It is signed by a John Stevenson and dated 2011, but it is unknown how or why this artwork came about. The building has been recognised for its historic significance, being recorded as a Category 2 building on the New Zealand Heritage List. Since this is one of the oldest remaining public toilets in New Zealand, it may well also be one of the country's most frequented flushers!

It is thought to be the city's first
women's public convenience block and
the only building built for the dual purpose
of sanitation and an electric tram shelter.

16

HOT WATER BEACH
PUBLIC TOILETS
Pye Place, Hot Water Beach 3510

An impressive new toilet block is no hot water for this beach.

Along with its dramatically beautiful seascape, Hot Water Beach's thermal water bubbling just beneath the surface of the sand has given the place cult-like status as a world-famous wonder. Armed with shovels and spades, and sporting rolled up sleeves and trouser legs, ready for work, visitors flock to the beach two hours either side of low tide to dig themselves a naturally thermal pool of water.

To accommodate the needs of the high number of international tourist visitors to the area in addition to the needs of surfers and local beach goers, the community, local council and public toilet provider Permaloo collaborated to come up with a number one solution for all the number ones and twos. The design brief was to

create an iconic beach amenity that was functional yet also creatively designed to stand out from the crowd. In 2017, such a facility was opened featuring unisex cubicles clad in natural timber, each with its own bench to facilitate use as a changing facility for two people. On the seaward side, an open, communal hand washing area allows for stunning views of the beach and sea.

...local council and public toilet provider Permaloo
collaborated to come up with
a number one solution for all
the number ones and twos.

17

HAHEI HOLIDAY RESORT, HAHEI

41 Harsant Ave, Hahei, Coromandel 3591

Reusing and recycling realises remarkable restrooms.

Located on New Zealand's iconic Coromandel Peninsula is the Hahei Holiday Resort. The resort offers a mix of camping, luxury accommodation and a glamping backpacker lodge designed to personify the eco beachfront coastal chic. To accommodate the scores of holidaymakers and backpackers, the toilet and shower block needed redesigning. A modest budget forced owners to think outside the square and upcycle what could be salvaged to create something quite special.

The new block has easy access ramps with sensor lighting, oversized showers and toilets and music piped 24/7 to soften the noise created from ... ahem ... bathroom experiences! A bright, coastal chic boathouse feel is created through the use of opaque clearlite roofing, open trusses and recycled timber. Designers CK Interior Design delivered on a 'reuse, recycle' brief, upcycling materials wherever

possible, including shelving and door handles made from on-site-aged felled trees, bespoke beer bottle light fittings that hang above the showers and loos, and ceramic sinks reclaimed from a hospital surgery department. The showstopper piece, though, might well be the gazebo waiting area that cleverly transforms that awkward, frustrating wait into a relaxing, social experience! The toilet facility was recognised for its brilliance, winning Best Design

in the 2017 International Toilet Tourism Award.

18

WAIHI BEACH PUBLIC TOILETS
24 Wilson Road, Waihi Beach, Bay of Plenty 3611

A see-through toilet?

Waihi Beach's 9-km stretch of sand is one of New Zealand's safest surf beaches and home to an inviting and friendly community. In the middle of the little Waihi Beach township, local artist Shane Walker worked his magic on a new toilet block that was installed in 2016. Shane's work captures the relaxed atmosphere of Waihi Beach using 3D features to create the illusion of an old, weathered, broken beach shack through which a coastal scene can be seen. Fortunately, although it appears that you can see through it, you can't see into it! Shane made sure to add a few perfect waves to entice keen surfers, and a touch of humour is added with the addition of a sunglass-wearing dog, which Shane based on his flatmate's little staffy named Rocki.

19

WAIHI BEACH SURF CLUB TOILETS

The Esplanade, Waihi Beach, Bay of Plenty 3611

Cisterns that celebrate the surf!

Founded in 1936, the Waihi Surf Life Saving Club provides the summer's hordes of beachgoers with patrolled swimming areas. Lots of beachgoers means lots of lots of demand for toilets! So, in 2014, Permaloo was engaged by the Western Bay of Plenty District council to create a custom-designed toilet block suited to the immediate surroundings.

The harsh coastal environment required the hardest-wearing materials, the high usage required it to be functional and easy to maintain and clean, especially for sand removal, and, being located adjacent to the surf club meant the design had to be iconic and something the community could be proud of. The finished result certainly delivered on these requirements. On approach from the carpark, the facility is discretely hidden by a huge coastal scene mural wrapped around the rear of the building, painted by local artist Shane Walker. The mono-pitched roof, supported by large laminated beams, is an impressive architectural structure on the beach side. But the standout features of this toilet block are the four unique outdoor showers that resemble surfboards set vertically in the sand.

20

DIGGELMANN PARK PUBLIC TOILETS
79 Main Rd,
Katikati 3129

A toilet inspired by the log!

Katikati holds the title 'Mural Capital of New Zealand', as the town is like an open-air art gallery celebrating the town's specific historical, cultural and environmental influences. So you might be forgiven for assuming that any toilet from this town featuring in this book would do so because of its elaborate and colourful mural. In fact, the toilet that has earned its place on the top toilets list is a primitive-looking toilet block, clad in rough-sawn timber and sitting modestly in Diggelmann Park.

The inspiration for the design begins to become clear as you walk around the park and read the information signs detailing the significance of the area's kauri logging past. The pretty water feature turns out to be a 1:10 scale replica of a simple kauri dam similar to those previously built in the area. And the toilet block is in fact a replica of an old logger's hut typical of those that once existed throughout the local Kaimai Mamaku Forest Park.

> In fact, the toilet that has earned its place on the top toilets list is a primitive-looking toilet block, clad in rough-sawn timber

The simple form of the hut's living area forms the main toilet block, and the steep mono-pitched roof of the old cooking and chimney area is an accessible cubicle entry foyer. The roof structure of corrugated steel and simple thatch is a nod to the utilitarian nature of the original huts that were, essentially, temporary housing of the day. While respect for the primitive loggers' huts of past is reflected in the exterior through using the original form and materials, inside reveals a modern purpose-built facility featuring one unisex cubicle with access for disabled users plus two conventional unisex cubicles. Here is one toilet where you can really appreciate logging!

21

SHEEPDOG PUBLIC TOILETS

Tirau i-SITE Visitor Information Centre, 65 Main Road, Tirau 3410

Mark your territory at this doggy loo!

Great cafés and an extensive range of boutique shops and art and craft stores make the quaint town of Tirau a popular stopping place for travellers. And there are enough reasons here to stick around for long enough to feel the urge to visit two different corrugated iron toilet masterpieces.

Built in 1998, a huge sheepdog sits impressively on the roadside. It conceals the i-SITE visitor centre and has a toilet accessible 24/7 sitting just under its left ear. Steven Clothier, a mechanic by trade, designed the structure, and, with the help of his dairy farmer friend, Tom Langland, the façade was built by hand with tin snips and a hand riveter. This iconic landmark put Tirau on the map and gave the town the title 'Corrugated Capital of the World'. Out of his studio, Corrugated Creations, Steven went on to craft thousands more creations of all shapes and sizes with this roofing material. Steven is now affectionately known as the 'Tin Man of Tirau', and many more of his corrugated iron pieces have continued to be added around Tirau since, including cabbage trees, a pukeko and a shepherd. The sheepdog now herds an equally enormous ram and sheep, which house a wool and craft store.

22

OUTHOUSE PUBLIC TOILETS

3 Hillcrest Street, Tirau, 3410

Feel a little flushed sitting in full display!

Tirau's Outhouse opened in 2017 to provide an alternative convenient stop for visitors! Tirau's Tin Man, Steven Clothier, was of course involved in this corrugated creation. Steven made use of rusted corrugated iron on these delightful dunnies to capture the authentic look and feel of an outhouse. What makes these a true tourist attraction, though, is the humorous photo opportunity allowing visitors to snap a picture of themselves on the job while reading the newspaper! You can actually read an article about Steven and the creation of the sheepdog in this newspaper, the Corrugated Courier. Thankfully, the outhouse's exterior façade is not continued inside – you'll enjoy modern and clean facilities with flushing toilets!

23

THE REDWOODS SHROUD ART TOILETS

The Redwoods, Whakarewarewa Forest, Rotorua 3074

Going back to nature can enhance a call of nature!

Known to locals as 'The Redwoods', the beautiful 5,600 hectares of Whakarewarewa Forest is just five minutes from central Rotorua. The area, with its continually evolving forest trails, can be enjoyed by walking, biking, horse riding or just relaxing under the canopy of majestic trees. For a unique perspective of the

...a fusion of Māori kowhaiwhai patterns and iconic, contemporary native bird images...

native undergrowth, visitors can walk The Redwoods' 553-metre long treewalk which reaches up to 12 metres above ground via its twenty-one suspension bridges traversing the forest. At night, the forest walk is transformed into a magical,

lantern-lit wonderland. Illuminated by infinite colour spots, feature lights and thirty bespoke lanterns courtesy of world-acclaimed designer David Trubridge, the Redwoods Nightlights is a beautifully unique nocturnal experience.

Nestled sympathetically within this forest of Californian redwoods, a collection of cylindrical structures shrouding toilets emerges. These shrouds, designed by Darryl Church of DCA Architects, resemble sturdy tree trunks, with the exteriors being cleverly made from weathered corten steel to be camouflaged within the forest. Following a call for art submissions, Māori artist Kereama Taepa's design was chosen to decorate

each metal cylinder. His art, a fusion of Māori kowhaiwhai patterns and iconic, contemporary native bird images, appropriately compliments the forest theme.

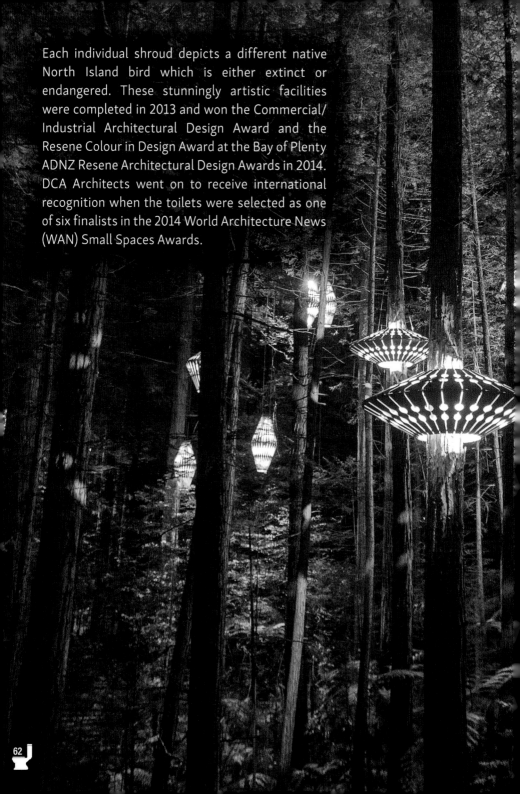

Each individual shroud depicts a different native North Island bird which is either extinct or endangered. These stunningly artistic facilities were completed in 2013 and won the Commercial/ Industrial Architectural Design Award and the Resene Colour in Design Award at the Bay of Plenty ADNZ Resene Architectural Design Awards in 2014. DCA Architects went on to receive international recognition when the toilets were selected as one of six finalists in the 2014 World Architecture News (WAN) Small Spaces Awards.

24

WAIPA VALLEY BIKE PARK PUBLIC TOILETS
Waipa State Mill Road (off SH5), Rotorua 3074

No need to dig a toilet hole here – it's already been done for you!

Rotorua is the biking capital of New Zealand, and thousands of locals and visitors ride the fantastic Whakarewarewa Forest's 180-kilometre trail network every year. Waipa Valley provides a recreational gateway into the Whakarewarewa Forest, in particular for mountain biking. Developing this area into a mountain bike hub has already resulted in building twin toilet and shower blocks. The facilities are cleverly concealed, being cut into either side of what resembles a hobbit hill with a mountain bike track running over the top. Far from being a toilet hole (or, to use the correct term, pit latrine), these blocks are fully functional and

well maintained, featuring twelve unisex toilets, four showers, changing space and provision for disabled users.

Metal artwork panels on both of the blocks feature artist Kereama Taepe's modern Māori designs. His kowhaiwhai patterns incorporate images of dragonflies and cicadas to reference the forest, and bike chains and gear spokes to reference the dominant use of the area. Near-future plans for the area include a world-class BMX track facility, a hot tub bathing and spa development and a commercial complex.

Whether using the area for walking, biking or relaxing, consider coming here armed with the joke:

Q: Why did the toilet roll bike down the hill?

A: He wanted to reach the bottom!

25

LAKE TIKITAPU (BLUE LAKE) PUBLIC TOILETS

Lake Tikitapu Scenic Reserve, Tarawera Road, Rotorua 3040

A loo looking out to a legendary lake.

Lake Tikitapu (Blue Lake) lies next to Rotokakahi (Green Lake), and Māori legend has it that this pristinely clean and beautiful blue lake was once inhabited by a taniwha (water monster). The perimeter walking and biking tracks allow for various vantage points to view the lake, while the water itself is popular with water-skiers and boaties. Following a call for artists from the Rotorua Lakes Council in 2015 to enhance the lakeside toilet block, several submissions were received from muralists. A community-based selection panel chose the final designs for the five panels that conceal the toilet block. On the inside, Tom Wallace, from Wellington, celebrates the wide range of native and endemic bird life in the area with boldly coloured, close-up bird portraits. On the exterior of the panels, Shane Walker's moody and mystic landscape design appears to almost mirror the lake scene. Shane wanted to encapsulate the lake's spiritual energy that he felt there, 'especially post-storm when the bush and ranges are laden with mist'.[1]

26

OTOROHANGA PUBLIC TOILETS

Bell Lane, Otorohanga 3900

*Dunny get stuck for synonyms
at this thesaurus throne!*

Otorohanga is New Zealand's Kiwiana capital – a celebration of New Zealand's popular culture. You've only to take a walk down the Ed Hillary walkway in the centre of town with its Kiwiana Arcade full of murals, sculptures and displays to appreciate Kiwi icons, heritage and heroes. The town is simply full of Kiwiana, and even the public toilets are a tribute to the theme. The exterior of the 'his and hers' block is emblazoned with traditional and Kiwi slang names for toilets. Inside, the toilet walls are decorated with local arty tiles, giving them an Otorohanga personal feel.

Dunny

The Throne

Bog

MEN

Drop Zone

Outhouse

Can

Longdrop

(accessible and men restroom symbols)

27

BENNEYDALE PUBLIC TOILETS

34 Ellis Road (Hwy 30), Benneydale, King Country, Waikato 3987

Take a tinkle before the Timber Trail!

Deep within the Pureora Forest, between Lake Taupo and Te Kuiti, the 85-km-long Timber Trail weaves through ancient forests, across ancestral lands of local Māori tribes, and along part of the historic Ongarue Tramway. It boasts some of New Zealand's highest and longest suspension bridges.

In response to the growing popularity of this walking and cycle track, a brand spanking new toilet block was installed in Benneydale, the gateway to the Timber Trail. The toilet installation, provided by Permaloo in 2017, features a huge wrap-around mural painted by Taupo local Gary Bennett. Gary took three weeks to complete the artwork, which showcases the trail's beauty and uses. Gary made a last-minute decision to include an image of two cyclists taking a selfie, which successfully positions the design in the twenty-first century.

The toilet installation, provided by Permaloo in 2017, features a huge wrap-around mural painted by Taupo local Gary Bennett. Gary took three weeks to complete the artwork...

28

HIPAPATUA/REID'S FARM RECREATION RESERVE

Huka Falls Road, Taupo 3330

Go with the flow of the river!

The Taupo region is a popular tourist destination boasting the beautiful waters of the largest freshwater lake in Australasia, Lake Taupo. With a backdrop of snow-peaked, volcanic mountains, the lake provides a perfect setting for walking, cycling and picnicking, and is nature's finest playground for swimming, boating and trout fishing.

Located on the banks of the crystal clear, blue waters of the Waikato River between the township of Taupo and Huka Falls, Reid's Farm Recreation Reserve has also long been a popular site for camping, fishing, picnicking and kayaking. Recently, the name Hipapatua has been adopted for the area to signify the area's cultural heritage. The name translates to 'waka landing' and reflects the intended use of the area for recreation and as a stopping point for people to stay for a short time.

High numbers of campers and visitors created a need for better toilet facilities, but, with no power and a tricky site to navigate, this was no easy feat. Using existing vault tanks, Permaloo overcame the challenges, creating a level concrete platform on which to place a three-pan, dry vault toilet that utilised its own ventilation system to eliminate odours for the busy facilities. Overlooking the banks of the river, the exterior blank concrete walls were the perfect canvas for local artist Gary Bennett to create a beautiful wrap-around mural that depicts the views from these loos.

TAUPO CENTRAL PUBLIC TOILETS

119 Tongariro Street,
Taupo 3330

A satisfying stop for saddle-sore cyclists!

Artist Gary Bennett painted a cycle-themed mural on this toilet block on Tongariro Street, central Taupo. The Lake Taupo Cycle Challenge, held in November each year, is New Zealand's largest cycling event, drawing around 6,000 riders. Riders select from a variety of on- or off-road challenges including the options of cycling around the entire 160-km lake perimeter road track. If that isn't far enough, 'enduro' riders can opt to complete the circuit twice, four times and even eight times in the 1,280-km event! Gary painted his mural on the toilet block which marks the start and finish line of this event. It is cleverly designed to look correct when a pedestrian or motorist approaches at a 45-degree angle.

EMPORIUM EATERY AND BAR

2 Tennyson St, Napier South, Napier 4110

*It wasn't baroque, but they fixed
it anyway ... art deco style!*

Napier's art deco architecture, built after much of the city was destroyed in the 1931 Hawke's Bay earthquake, makes the town a tourist attraction in its own right, with tourists flocking to the city each year for its five-day art deco festival. Another highlight is Marine Parade, a tree-lined ocean boulevard that is essentially a playground for locals and visitors, with attractions that include sunken gardens, the iconic Spirit of Napier fountain, a spa complex, the National Aquarium, kids adventure play areas, mini-golf and a skate park.

The Emporium Eatery and Bar is a multiple award-winning venue that forms part of the beautifully refurbished 1932 original, iconic, art deco Masonic Hotel. The building has quite a history. Originally built in 1861, it burned down in 1896

before being rebuilt in 1897. The fires triggered by the 1931 earthquake claimed this building again before its rebuild in 1932. The Emporium Eatery and Bar opened in 2012, coinciding with a refurbishment of the hotel to bring it back to its former art deco glory. Owners Neil Barber and Craig Hay, who were instrumental in overseeing the restoration, contracted designer Tom Skyring, who blended the modern with the classic using opulent materials and elegant styling to create the perfect amount of art deco. His attention to detail meant that even the restrooms were appropriately designed and decorated. High-gloss black doors with gold art deco font, black and white chess-board-look

floor tiles and a wooden twin basin vanity create the bold, modern, geometric and refined look typical of art deco style. They say, 'If it's not baroque, don't fix it' (or something very similar anyway) – so thank goodness it's art deco!

31

BAY SKATE

290 Marine Parade, Napier South, Napier 4110

Home to the toilet bowl and overflow pipe,
and the skateboard bowl and half-pipe.

Bay Skate is a multi-use, world-class roller sports park on Napier's Marine Parade. The park's flat rink, ramps and concrete bowls cater for skateboarding, BMX, scootering, inline hockey, roller-skating, artistic skating and rollerblading.

The park also happens to be home to a fantastic piece of artwork on its toilet block! The art forms part of a series of large-scale murals created for Napier's Sea Walls: Artists for Oceans 2017 festival. The festival brought together many internationally renowned artists to enhance the town's streetscapes while highlighting the beauty of our oceans and addressing environmental issues. New Zealand-based artist Cracked Ink was chosen for the project at Bay Skate. His graffiti-style, comic-character-based art is bold and eye-catching and sits comfortably in the skate park surrounds. Titled Ocean Health the piece sends a strong message to stop overfishing and polluting the ocean.

32

CLIFTON ROAD RESERVE PUBLIC TOILETS
Clifton Road, Haumoana, Hastings, Hawke's Bay 4102
Toilets flushed with success!

Located on the beachfront Clifton Road Reserve between the settlements of Haumoana and Te Awanga, this toilet block has come up trumps on more than one occasion! Keep New Zealand Beautiful declared the public toilets the best loos in the country for 2015. It was then awarded Best Small Project in the Gisborne/Hawke's Bay Regional Architecture Awards in 2016. The practical and robust building was designed to be seen and to frame the scenery – beautiful Cape Kidnappers, the sea and the trees.

The bold red colour was purposely chosen to connect with the pohutukawa trees,...

The bold red colour was purposely chosen to connect with the pohutukawa trees, and large sweeping lines cut into the panels playfully form huge, yet indiscernible, 'WC' inscriptions on each side of the building. Admit it, you didn't notice the WC letters until you read this – but now that you know, you can't un-see them! Their popular beachfront location means they are well used and they provide a welcome stop for cyclists using the coastal cycle path.

33

JAILHOUSE PUBLIC TOILET

Bridge Street, OngaOnga, Hawkes Bay 4278

Take a 'cell-fie' at this jailhouse john!

The little village of OngaOnga is a slice of local pioneering history with its collection of historic buildings that form an open-air museum. The OngaOnga Museum was established in 1966 around the town's old school building, which was built in 1875. It has grown over the years to include a restored 1912 butcher's shop, a wool shed, a military hut, a pioneer hut and a pioneer cottage built in 1876 for the matron of the local hospital. An old jailhouse from nearby Waipukurau was also originally part of the museum, but in 1996 it was moved to its present place on Bridge Street where it fulfils a new duty as OngaOnga's public toilet. Once a place where inmates were punished, it's now the porcelain that gets punished in these toilets that still feature jail bars at the windows and heavy metal peepholes in the doors. It's one toilet where you should make time to spend time doing time spending a penny.

Once a place where inmates were punished, it's now the porcelain that gets punished in these toilets

34

TONGARIRO ALPINE CROSSING TOILETS

Tongariro National Park, Manawatu-Wanganui 4691

Cleverly camouflaged khazis!

The 19.4-km Tongariro Alpine Crossing is a World Heritage site and is often heralded as New Zealand's best one-day hike. Completing a 765-metre climb that incorporates the aptly named Devil's Staircase, and then descending 1,125 metres, you'll be rewarded for your efforts with dynamic scenery, unique geological features and awe-inspiring, spectacular vistas, including the volcanic peaks of Ngauruhoe, Tongariro and Ruapehu. All three volcanoes are still active and have erupted in recent times!

For your own 'personal eruptions' along the way, you'll need to play 'I Spy' to find the toilets, as these Department of Conservation (DOC) long drops are all cleverly camouflaged to merge with their surroundings. To minimise the visual impact of the toilets, photographers visited the exact sites of each long drop toilet to take pictures of the views, which became life-sized vinyl wrappings for the external walls. Although they are unsurprisingly basic inside, some of these loos have incredible views.

Due the remoteness of these toilets, helicopters were required for installation. Helicopters are also needed to transport human waste in flyable tanks every 2–4 weeks at a cost of over $70,000 per summer. In other words, DOC are quite literally cleaning up other people's sh*t! And that's some expensive sh*t! In addition to the permanent toilets, additional temporary toilets are added at the top of Devil's Staircase and Blue Lake Saddle during the summer months to cope with demand, meaning that facilities are located at least every 90 minutes apart. Very convenient conveniences! These temporary toilets get removed over winter due to the high altitude and exposure at these alpine sites.

35

WAIOURU PUBLIC TOILETS
SH1 (opposite the National Army Museum), Waiouru 4861

Top toilets winning the Battle of WaterLoos!

Waiouru is the southern entry point to the Tongariro National Park and the last pit stop before the Desert Road. Situated across the road from the National Army Museum, the once dull dunnies failed to meet general standards (let alone military requirements), prompting action from the Ruapehu District Council. Mimicking the museum's fortress-looking building, the striking architectural design of this toilet block is based on the concept of a bunker. Having become an attractive stop-off, with gardens and picnic tables out the front, travellers are now relieved to find supremely clean, modern and spacious facilities. Indeed, the Central Plateau town's public toilets are undeniably ones the nation can be proud of, having defeated the competition and won the battle for Best Loo category in the 2016 Keep New Zealand Beautiful Awards.

Situated across the road from the National Army Museum, the once dull dunnies failed to meet general standards (let alone military requirements),

36

STRATFORD PUBLIC TOILETS

278 Broadway, Stratford 4332

Good toilet, good toilet.
Farting is such sweet sorrow.

Ok, they're not quite the words used by Shakespeare's Juliet to say goodnight to her lover, Romeo, but then again, these toilets are not actually in Shakespeare's Stratford-upon-Avon, they're in the Taranaki town of Stratford. Stratford, or to give the town its full name, Stratford-upon-Patea, honours the great playwright's birthplace and was so called due to its similarity to Stratford-Upon-Avon in England. Sixty-seven streets here have a reference to characters from Shakespeare's plays.

... at 10am, 1pm, 3pm and 7pm each day, clockwork figurines of Romeo and Juliet declare their love for one another.

The toilets are located beside the town's famous glockenspiel clock tower where at 10am, 1pm, 3pm and 7pm each day, clockwork figurines of Romeo and Juliet declare their love for one another. To complement the Shakespearian theme of the tower, the toilets' faux wattle and daub exterior resembles a Tudor building.

37

ELTHAM PUBLIC TOILETS
85–102 King Edward Street, Eltham, Taranaki 4322

The cheesy toilets at Eltham are full on flavour!

The long-held cheesemaking tradition of Eltham is sandwiched in the design of its public toilets, with a yellow, holey, cheese-themed veranda supported by recycled vintage iron columns. Inspired by the Hundertwasser public toilets in Kawakawa, architect Bill Jackson conceptualised these facilities to be similarly ornate and arty. The interior features an eclectic mix of leadlight window art, wrought ironwork, and tiling artwork and mosaics from Eltham's locals. The exterior corrugated iron artworks reflect the town's popular Kite Day and Trolley Derby Day in a style that complements its Edwardian and Victorian history. With the goal of encouraging more visitors to stop in this lovely little town, the Eltham Community Development Group worked with the Eltham Community Board to fundraise $80,000 for the restroom revamp, which was opened in 2015. And why wouldn't you want to stop here? Take a trip through time walking along Bridge Street with its heritage buildings. Browse for vintage and retro wares. And buy your favourite cheeses at the local cheese bar.

> The interior features an eclectic mix
> of leadlight window art, wrought ironwork,
> and tiling artwork and mosaics
> from Eltham's locals.

FOR YOUR CONVENIENCE
THESE TOILETS WILL BE
UNLOCKED AT DAWN
AND LOCKED AT DUSK

38

TUI HQ CAFÉ

Tui Brewery, 5 Mara Street (Off State Hwy 2), Mangatainoka, 4982

You can organise a p*ss-up in a brewery.

Driving through the bustling (Yeah right) town of Mangatainoka, the unmissable and unmistakable sight of the iconic Tui Tower is a sure sign that a cold beer is close at hand. This is the home of Tui – New Zealand's very own home-grown beer. The brewery boasts that they've been 'brewing legends since 1889', and this is one claim they don't follow with their trademark, sarcastic add-on, 'Yeah right'. Here, you can take a personalised 40-minute guided tour around Tui Brewery, trace the brewery's 125-year history and enjoy the Tui Tower yarn that explains how such a tall building ended up lacking a few crucial elements ... like stairs! A few too many beers on the job for the builders maybe?!

Round off the tour in the Tui HQ brewery bar tasting beers of your choice straight from the tap. There's a great selection of good, honest pub food and a vast beer garden to enjoy on sunny days. The Tui Brewery Bar's 'spit and sawdust' décor is easily appreciated, and although there may have been little expense needed in the design of their famous dunnies for 'Rams' and Ewes', you have to admire their simple ingenuity. The process, it appears, was:

Step 1: Take a beer keg.

Step 2: Chop the top off, smoothing any rough edges.

Step 3: Ta-da! You have a urinal!

Or, a Step 3: Ta-da! You have a hand basin!

The décor is finished off with a good coat of Tui Orange paint ... of course!

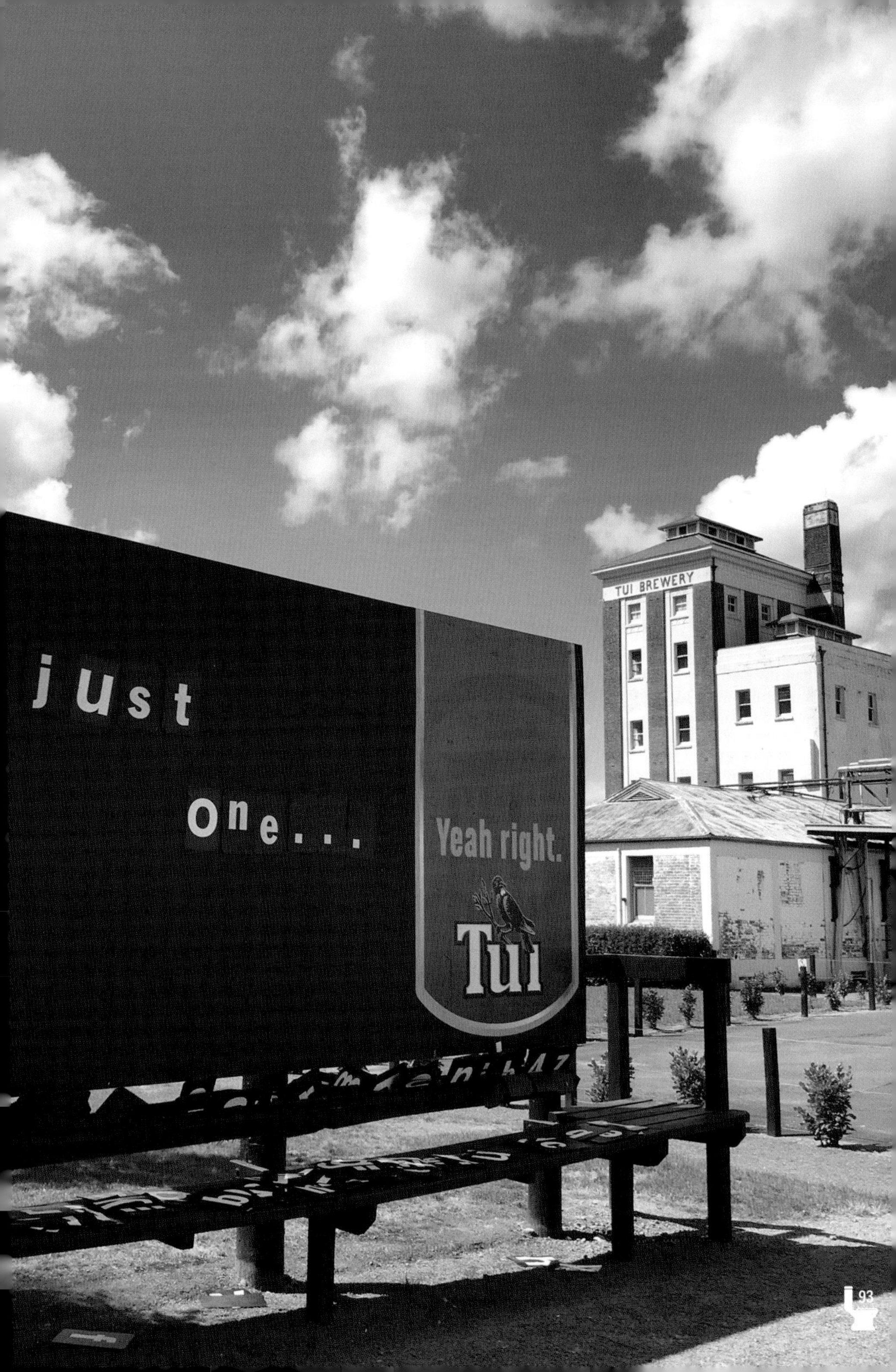
just
one...
Yeah right.
Tui
TUI BREWERY

39

KUMUTOTO PUBLIC TOILETS
59 Customhouse Quay, Wellington, 6011.
There's nothing bog-standard about these designer dunnies!

In New Zealand's compact, cool and cosmopolitan little capital city, there is no shortage of things to see and do. Join many other Wellingtonians walking, jogging, skating, cycling or crocodile biking along the waterfront promenade, which is dotted with parks, sculptures, cafés and bars. Continue into the centre to Cuba Street with its Bucket Fountain, street entertainers and colourful array of hip bars, cafés and vintage shops. And no trip to Wellington is complete without either taking the iconic, red Wellington Cable Car ride to the lookout or visiting the national museum of New Zealand, Te Papa. With free admission, Te Papa is fascinatingly fun for everyone and features innovative and often interactive exhibits year round.

While there, if you asked for directions to the nearest toilet, the alien-like creature that awaits you as you turn the corner from Queen's Wharf is hardly what you would expect to encounter. Being suggestive of sea crustaceans, and with a unisex toilet hidden within each of two red–orange elongated tentacles, it's easy to see why the toilets have been nicknamed the 'Lobster Loos'.

Following a competition brief to design something creative, practical and in a structural form that would be locally and nationally recognised, architect Bret Thurston's winning design delivers on all aspects. Both the colour and the design of the instantly recognisable structure fits surprisingly well within the surrounding heritage buildings and waterfront location. The toilets were built in 2011 and came with a hefty price tag of $375,000. However, they achieved the council's aim of raising the city's profile, having attracted plenty of international attention and even being crowned third best public toilets in the world for 2015 by DesignCurial.

40

FORK AND BREWER

14 Bond Street, Central Wellington, 6011

There's definitely something brewing in the toilets!

The people at Fork and Brewer in central Wellington take food and beer so seriously they used it in their name. A choice of forty tap beers are offered from the giant barrel bar, and all of the dishes have been carefully paired with one of their own craft beers using contrasting and complementary flavours to create what they call the 'perfect marriage of food and beer'.[2] To showcase their beer even further, Fork and Brewer make it in full sight of the customers in a custom-built brewery which bubbles away in the corner of the building.

Director Colin Mallon was determined to transform the boring box-shaped building that houses the Fork and Brewer into something that reflected their creativity in brewing. Wood features extensively in the floors, furniture and the imposing central barrel bar to offset the harsh steel beams and modern glass windows. Many of the hanging light fittings throughout the venue have been upcycled from offcuts generated by the rebuild and from wood found in the rafters. Colin also repurposed many of his own kitchen utensils as taps on the bar – apparently his wife was NOT impressed! And when you feel the need to recycle all the beer you have consumed, you won't be disappointed with the toilets. To seamlessly carry the wood aspect and the service of alcohol through to the toilets, wooden barrels have been repurposed into

hand basins. Colin also opted against generic signage for the toilets, finding an appropriately alternative and amusing use for Ken and Barbie dolls, which are recessed into the entrance to the toilets.

Colin also repurposed many of his
own kitchen utensils as taps
on the bar – apparently his wife
was NOT impressed!

SOUTH ISLAND

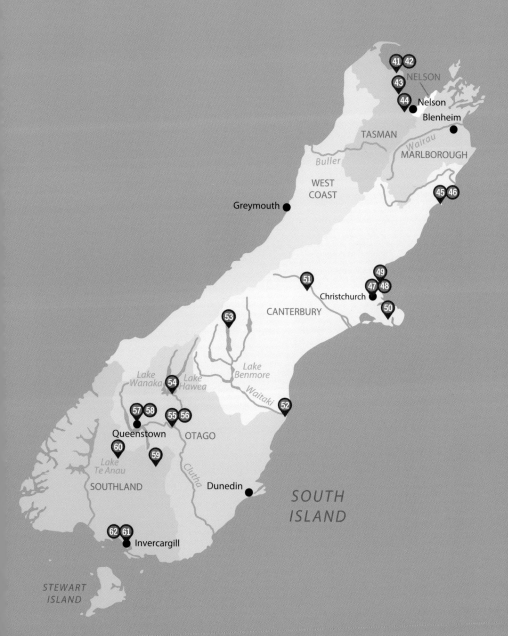

NELSON

TASMAN

Wairau

Buller

MARLBOROUGH

WEST
COAST

Greymouth ●

Nelson

Blenheim ●

CANTERBURY

Christchurch ●

*Lake
Benmore*

Waitaki

*Lake
Wanaka*

*Lake
Hawea*

Queenstown

OTAGO

Clutha

*Lake
Te Anau*

SOUTHLAND

Dunedin ●

SOUTH
ISLAND

Invercargill

*STEWART
ISLAND*

41

MUSSEL INN
1259 SH60, Onekaka, Golden Bay 7182

Toilets as 'Kiwi as' as the 'Kiwi as' venue!

It's an old, single-room building clad with corrugated iron. It's on a corner in the middle of nowhere. It's simple. It's basic. It's 'Kiwi as'. And yet it is hugely popular, attracting customers and musicians from around the world. Built in 1992, the Mussel Inn is a pub and performance venue located in the heart of Golden Bay that resembles a 'Kiwi woolshed/tramping hut meets Aussie farmhouse'.[3]

The design and ethos of the place reflect the ideals of owners Jane and Andrew Dixon, who are self-confessed 'green hippies'. Facing the challenge of a finite water supply, prioritising this precious resource for making beer over flushing toilets was a no-brainer for Andrew. What he needed was a no-flush facility.

Andrew had already installed a composting toilet, which had been designed and manufactured in the United States, in their home. However, he felt the unit had a few shortcomings and wanted something that would be easy to maintain, did not require electricity, could be retro-fitted in existing buildings, and, most importantly, could handle any 'loading rate'. So he designed one. Made a few. Installed some in the Mussel Inn. Sold a lot more of them. Then on-sold the whole operation! Andrew may be a hippy, but this hippy is quite the entrepreneur!

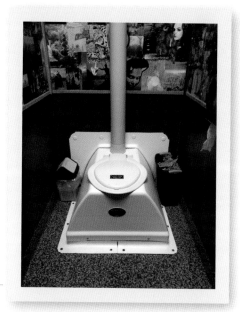

The design and ethos of the place reflect the ideals of owners Jane and Andrew Dixon, who are self-confessed hippies.

Andrew reckons the Mussel Inn toilets (called Kakapo toilets) have probably done the equivalent of at least a hundred years of domestic use and are still going strong. 'Where does it all go?' I hear you ask. The answer is: Kakapo juice. Andrew turns it into Kakapo juice! But, before you swear never to drink juice at the Mussel Inn again, rest assured. It's juice for his gardens,

which he says are wonderfully lush and healthy. Does everything compost? Apparently not! Thanks to plastic bank notes, Andrew has found, among other non-degradable items, the odd $50 note. Note to self: when ordering from the bar, tell them to keep the change, thank you!

POHARA PUBLIC TOILETS, POHARA

876 Abel Tasman Drive, Pohara, Golden Bay 7183

Where penguin privies are public potties!

The doors on these two toilets are painted with caricatures of the resident little blue penguins that have made this part of New Zealand their home. Here, the 26-km curve of Farewell Spit, the largest spit in NZ, protects them from the fury of the Pacific Ocean. However, while these comical characters may well welcome you to wee, there are disappointingly dull dunnies inside.

TAKAKA PUBLIC TOILETS, TAKAKA
16 Willow Street, Takaka, Tasman 7110

You'll be a shadow of your former self after using these loos!

Located at the entry to the colourful and alternative township of Takaka in Golden Bay, this toilet block is strikingly obvious. Using a simple form made from concrete blocks and a floating mono-pitched roof, the bold colour scheme and comically designed metal screen complement Takaka's arty (or arty-farty in this case!) reputation. Appearing almost like part of a child's paper-doll chain, the smiling silhouettes of a male and female, made of black powder-coated steel, stand at the entrance of three unisex toilets, casting a shadow on the floor and doors behind them.

Designed by local Arthouse Architects, this outhouse is an arthouse too. The toilet block impressed judges at the 2002 New Zealand Institute of Architects, and received an award for its architecturally unique design and a Colour Award for its strong palette, which judges said helps to dispel the embarrassment associated with public toilets.

JESTER HOUSE CAFÉ, MOTUEKA

320 Aporo Road, Motueka, Tasman 7173

The Jester's composting toilets are no joke!

Jester House seems to capture the essence of the Nelson area with its quirky charm, beautifully imaginative garden setting, superb food and friendly service. The café specialises in serving delicious food made on site using locally sourced, fresh, organic and artisan ingredients, and offers great beers from the Mussel Inn and wines from local vineyards. The inside feels like a magical fairy-tale cottage and the garden wonderland is full of unique play areas and arty surprises.

Jester House gained notoriety by taking out New Zealand's Café of the Year in 2013. However, the café's fame has quite possibly grown just as much from having tame eels in the creek. Here you can observe the eels in their natural setting and hand feed them from a stick (food and stick provided by the café).

Whereas many stories of toilet upgrades describe transitioning from long drops to ones with fancy flush mechanisms, when owners Judy and Steve Richards rebuilt the Jester House Café in 2006, they took the opportunity to upgrade to composting toilets. In keeping with their eco-building and eco-philosophy, they wanted something that turned waste into a resource. The property pumps its own water, and, since splash toilets are heavy water users (especially in a commercial situation), composting toilets were a great way to reduce waste water. Finding a toilet that provided a solution was surprisingly easy – it helps when your brother who lives nearby has designed his own composting toilet for his own business, the Mussel Inn! The toilets work as a compost collection, and the materials are then taken to a hot compost bin system to complete the compost process, which takes 6–8 months. The resulting compost is used in their large permaculture garden (a garden that uses free, sustainable energies and resources).

While this description may paint a picture of dingy, basic and smelly facilities, the toilet cubicles are charming, inviting and surprisingly odour-free. There are tool shed-themed cubicles for the men and beautifully decorated powder rooms for the ladies. You could be forgiven for not realising they were composting toilets until you read the instructions on the wall. That's right ... instructions!

Complete with the advice 'Don't be scared'! Apparently, people are occasionally afraid to use them and ask if there is another toilet. There is. Another composting toilet! Maybe they're not to everyone's liking. But then again, maybe if people are that uptight, their sh*t wouldn't compost anyway?!

45

KAIKOURA TOWN CENTRE PUBLIC TOILETS

49 West End, Kaikoura Central, Canterbury 7300

From drab to rehab.

A common colourful theme becomes apparent as you walk through Kaikoura. Fed up with what they felt was a drab town centre, retired residents Jean Laming and Marie Scott set about brightening up Kaikoura. So now, brightly coloured murals of the same ilk decorate the local school, swimming pool, bowling club and, of course, the toilets!

Using paint supplied by the council, in 2014 the two ladies took approximately two weeks to transform the town centre's toilets with a mural depicting everything that Kaikoura represents: whales, dolphins, seals, the ocean, mountains, tourists, kids, old people, Māori and farming. Artist Jean, an experienced muralist, took the lead, painting the walls freehand using designs she held in her head with assistance from Marie. The two ladies also painted another toilet mural beside the town's playground that playfully pokes fun at the length of time often required when queuing outside the female toilets. It features a long line of 'desperately needing to go' women compared to a relaxed-looking, solitary man. The ladies consider their work to be a colourful gift to the community.

46

SOUTH END PUBLIC TOILETS
Kaikoura Peninsular Walkway, Kaikoura, Canterbury 7300

A very pukka wharepaku!

This impressive peninsular walkway hugs the coastline and provides walkers with cliff top views of the sea with a mountainous backdrop. Wildlife, including whales, dolphins, seals and birds, may be spotted along the way. The walkway passes through land administered or owned by several organisations – Te Rūnanga o Ngāi Tahu, Te Rūnanga o Kaikōura, Kaikoura District Council, Whale Watch Kaikoura and the Department of Conservation – all of whom formed part of a planning group to oversee its improvements.

As part of enhancements to the walkway, toilets at South Bay were built in 2006. The toilet block and adjoining information shelter were designed by Daines Matz Architecture and cost just over $200,000. The information shelter has a long slit to resemble a whaler's lookout, which reflects the whaling history of the area, framing the seaview like a picture.

The information shelter has a long slit to resemble a whaler's lookout, which reflects the whaling history of the area, framing the seaview like a picture.

47

MARGARET MAHY PLAYGROUND
177 Armagh St, Christchurch Central, Christchurch 8011

Tatty patchwork toilets that are not so shabby!

These toilets are part of the elaborately designed Margaret Mahy Family Playground located on the edge of the Avon River in Christchurch's city centre. Forming part of the Christchurch Rebuild anchor projects following the 2011 earthquake, the playground is inspired by, and named after, New Zealand's most acclaimed children's writer, Margaret Mahy (1936–2012).

The colourful playground opened in December 2015 and is the largest playground in the southern hemisphere. Being the result of the Christchurch Central Development Unit's Amazing Place playground design competition, the playground is ultimately designed by children for children, so it is of no surprise that it is a child's utopia! It features a 40-metre-long double flying fox, a 4-metre-wide

slide, a gigantic climbing tower with curly-whirly slide, water play areas and a spider-climbing net.

The playground's toilet block exterior is decorated with artwork by Canterbury children, generated in response to a Tremendous Tatty Patchwork competition. Each 'patch' of artwork is inspired by the child's surroundings and beautifully meets the competition's 'creative, colourful and Cantabrian' brief.[4] Fittingly, the competition and resulting collaborative artwork echoes the work of two of Margaret Mahy's characters: Selina and her grandmother, Mrs Polly, who created amazing patchworks in 'The Tatty Patchwork Rubbish Dump Dancers' (from The Chewing Gum Rescue and other stories). The modern facilities are touch-button locked, operate sensor-controlled flushing and hand washing, talk to you upon entering and play soft music to accompany your movements! Be warned though … you may have a wee problem if you linger longer than 10 minutes, as they unlock automatically!

48

DUX CENTRAL

6 Poplar St, Christchurch Central, Christchurch 8011

Toilet signs that really take the p*ss!

The Dux is something of a Christchurch icon. Starting out in 1989 as Dux de Lux within the Christchurch Arts Centre, it became the place to eat, drink and enjoy music. The devastating 2011 Christchurch earthquake forced Dux de Lux

Trying to contain the involuntary, audible gasp as your senses fully appreciate the confronting photographs displayed on the male and female toilets' entrance doors is futile!

to relocate, but since it was impossible to find one all-encompassing spot to accommodate it as a restaurant, brewery and live music venue, the Dux diversified. Dux Central now fulfils some of the Dux's original concepts and comprises the Brew Bar, the Emerald Room, Upper Dux, the Courtyard and The Poplar Social Club. However, whether you are having a beer and enjoying the 'London pub' vibe of Brew Bar or sipping fine wine within the opulence and elegance of the Emerald Room, you will at some point want to locate and use Dux Central's unmistakable toilets.

Trying to contain the involuntary, audible gasp as your senses fully appreciate the confronting photographs displayed on the male and female toilets' entrance doors is futile! Covering the entire door for each toilet is a full-size silhouette of a person backlit to highlight ... well ... the exiting flow of urine. The letters 'M' and 'F' are included just in case there is any doubt as to what these pictures show! It's when comparing the relaxed posture of the male figure, leaning backwards in comfortable relief, with the physical feat required of the female to strongly hold the

squat position (who will clearly be experiencing slightly damp underwear, shoes and even ankles judging from the urine splashing back from the floor) that you can truly appreciate the female struggle!

Inside the facilities, just in case the men find the lack of effort required to relieve themselves a little boring, the urinals come complete with a computer game controlled by the flow of their urine. However, no such game appears in the ladies' toilets – although they are possibly too busy, anyway, drying their knickers with the hand dryer!

WUNDERBAR

19 London Street, Lyttelton 8082

Toilets so secret, you may pee yourself trying to find them!

Wunderbar translated is quite possibly the most wonderfully weird and weirdly wonderful bar in New Zealand. Sitting in the port of Lyttelton, this elusive bar is accessed via a supermarket or by climbing the exterior fire staircase found in a backstreet carpark! Whispers of Wunderbar have spread far and wide, with people coming from afar to see for themselves the oddity that is unveiled inside. Vintage purple sofas, fabric padded walls, and an absence of windows gives the place a retro nightclub vibe, irrespective of the time of day you visit. In every direction, the ceiling and walls are festooned with strange items and antiques, including

Whispers of Wunderbar have spread far and wide, with people coming from afar to see for themselves the oddity that is unveiled inside.

lightshades made from beheaded dolls, hair rollers (complete with strands of someone's hair) and old toilet brushes (thankfully minus any remnants of old!)

Speaking of toilets ... where are they? Legend has it that only the enlightened ones can find them. Among those who have tried and failed, one writes, 'Even after directions and bizarre hand signals from a Wunderian I still could not find them, panicking I soured and picked at the walls with my fingernails certain there must be some sort of hidden lever or something ...'[5]

So, to provide you with an insider's directions:
First, the foosball table you must find.
Ladies, reach for a domestic tool of the ironing kind.
Gentlemen must hold another's hand, there you shall reach the toilet promised land.

In other words, the doors are hidden among wall panels behind the foosball table – the ladies' door handle is an iron, the gents' is a fake hand!

50

HARBAR BEACH CAFÉ AND BAR
83 Rue Jolie, Akaroa 7520

Une vue pittoresque sur la mer à partir d'un joli, petit loo.
(A picturesque sea view from a pretty, little loo.)

You'll struggle to find a more picturesque view for a poo from a loo than this pew! Located in New Zealand's French settlement of Akaroa, the tiny HarBar Beach Café and Bar sits right on the water of the beautiful Akaroa Harbour. It accommodates just 60 guests, so it is unsurprising that there is a mere lone loo here. But disappointing it is not! The uninterrupted water view from the bar continues into the cute, beach bach-styled toilet. The partially translucent glass window protects your modesty but a full sea vista is appreciated when standing to wash your hands!

51

MT HUTT SKI AREA

Mt Hutt Skifield Access Rd, Mt Hutt, Canterbury 7782

The business that looks forward to huge dumps … (of snow)!

Mt Hutt has been no stranger to award winning, coming first in the New Zealand's Best Ski Resort category at the annual World Ski Awards in 2015, 2016 and 2017. But their crowning glory also extends to their thrones! Set at an altitude of 1610 m, they are literally 'top' toilets in New Zealand, and, after a major rebuild of their facilities, they also won Best Loo in the 2017 Keep New Zealand Beautiful awards.

There is no need to 'write your name in the snow' on the slopes here, with clean and modern facilities that are accessed through wide corridors featuring huge murals showcasing the ski fields on the main walls. To best accommodate the scores of skiers, the toilets were cleverly designed to be: 1) accessible from the snow and café areas – there's nothing worse than inconvenient conveniences! 2) spacious – each cubical is slightly longer and wider than the standard to ease the disrobing struggle that only skiers can relate to! and, 3) state of the art – self-flushing toilets, auto foam soap dispensers and airblade taps mean guests can 'go' almost as quickly as one could make yellow snow.

To create a cleaner footprint in the snow, the toilet revamp was preceded with a $120,000 sewerage treatment system upgrade to separate non-biological waste from ... well ... yellow snow and mountain boulders! A stroke of ingenuity also means that a substantial heat recovery system takes warm air being extracted from the toilets to heat the frigid incoming fresh air from outside.

The long-awaited toilet upgrade created much excitement from guests who couldn't wait for *their* first dump along with *the* first dump of snow! The toilets were such a big deal that 'First on the toilet' t-shirts were organised to match the 'First on the chair' t-shirts that are traditionally given out on the first day of each season.

Set at an altitude of 1610m, they are literally 'top' toilets in New Zealand.

52

FRIENDLY BAY PLAYGROUND TOILETS
Esplanade, South Hill, Oamaru 9400

Toilets in an area that transports you back to the futuristic past!

With some of New Zealand's best-preserved Victorian buildings, shopping in Oamaru's Victorian precinct, with its antique shops, vintage-clothing stores, artist studios and galleries, feels like you could be a character in one of Dickens' novels. The area has become the capital of steampunk – a fun genre of steam-powered science fiction set in an alternate, futuristic version of the Victorian period. If you're still struggling to understand the term steampunk, try imagining inventions that the Victorians might have created for the modern world. Still unsure? Then pay a visit to Steampunk HQ, an interactive museum featuring an interesting collection of everything steampunk.

Located at Oamaru Harbour's Friendly Bay, the playground forms part of Oamaru's steampunk wonderland. This quirky and uniquely exciting playground includes a penny farthing swing set, a Salvador Dali-esque giant armoured elephant with fireman's pole, a huge flying fox, a giant hamster wheel and a large roadmap for young children to safely navigate on their bikes. After an offer for 'steampunked toilets' was declined by the council, local architect Ian Perry designed these toilets using an idea from an Oamaru town landscaping plan which identified historic red sheds at the end of Oamaru's harbour. These toilets mirror these historic red sheds, effectively linking the park with Oamaru's historic waterfront and Victorian precinct. The facilities are therefore well suited to the area. However, you can't help but feel somewhat disappointed that they are not more 'steampunky'. Maybe toilets befitting a more futuristic past will exist here one day in the future?

These toilets mirror these historic red sheds, effectively linking the park with Oamaru's historic waterfront and Victorian precinct.

53

HOOKER VALLEY TRACK DOC TOILETS
Aoraki/Mt Cook National Park, 7999

*The view from this loo
will blow you away!*

The Aoraki/Mt Cook National Park is where you will find the country's longest glaciers and highest mountains, including, of course, the mighty 3724 m high Aoraki/Mt Cook itself. While mountaineers may regard the area as the best in Australasia, the incredible alpine scenery can be more easily appreciated from vantage points in Aoraki/Mt Cook Village or from some of the many walking tracks. The Hooker Valley Track is a popular 10-km track where

you'll be visually rewarded for your physical effort. The well-formed track leads up the Hooker Valley towards Aoraki/Mt Cook, criss-crossing over the Hooker River several times via impressive swing bridges. The return track ends at the glacier lake where you'll enjoy stunning views of Mt Cook, Hooker Glacier and the Southern Alps. Halfway along this walk sit two cylindrical DOC long drop toilets, camouflaged well into the environment. The most amazing mountain vista can be appreciated as you exit these basic bogs, meaning these truly are loos with the best views in NZ.

Top tip #1: the view is so amazing you'll want to leave the door open.

Top tip #2: It's a popular walk; you'll want to close the door!

54

PUZZLING WORLD
188 Wanaka-Luggate Hwy (Hwy 84), Wanaka 9382

U-bends that bend your mind!

Easily identified by its iconic wonky-house exterior, Puzzling World is a must-do attraction where the fun includes a 3D 'Super Maze', a large puzzle centre and café, and an incredible collection of illusion rooms. And Wanaka's wonderful world of weirdness certainly does not stop where the toilet block starts. The innovative design of the Roman toilets incorporates a diorama, painted by artist Sam Foley, depicting Roman men using a lavatorium that links seamlessly to an actual lavatorium recreated for people to sit on. The attention to construction and painting detail cleverly creates an illusionary opportunity for visitors where they appear to be sitting (or is it sh*tting?!) in the scene with the Romans. Thankfully, this very public public toilet is only a communal photographic experience within a waiting area between more private male and female toilet cubicles!

Even in the real restrooms, visitors continue to be entertained with illusions on the toilet door interiors and clear resin seats containing a bizarre variety of inanimate objects (bottle caps, coral, casino chips and more). The toilets are definitely worth visiting before you attempt the Super Maze. With an average of one hour required to complete the maze, you won't want to be caught short looking for short cuts!

If your mind needs bending further, two more puzzle abyss toilets are located within the illusionary rooms. The 3D anamorphic designs on the floors in these restrooms make it appear as though the ground is giving way as you make your way to the loo. Providing the most mind-bending experience you're likely to have while doing your business, the toilets at Puzzling World are next-level dunnies with a difference!

55

CROMWELL TOWN CENTRE PUBLIC TOILET AND BUS SHELTER
Lode Lane, Cromwell, Otago 9310

Sweet-as toilets in 'The fruit bowl of the South'.

Serving a dual function of bus shelter and toilet block, these facilities were opened in 2012. Mary Jowett Architects Ltd designed the toilet block with oxidised steel and cut stone to connect with both the Old Cromwell Historic Precinct and Central Otago's rocky landscape. The rusted screens which provide privacy and shelter for bus passengers feature a cut out cherry-leaf-shape detail that is also used on the town's welcome sign and reflects the areas' fruit growing association. While this is eye-catching during the day, at night the back lighting creates an even more dramatic effect. The facilities received a Southern Architecture Award in 2013 in the Small Project Architecture category.

> While this is eye-catching during the day, at night the back lighting creates an even more dramatic effect.

56

CROMWELL HERITAGE PRECINCT PUBLIC TOILET

(Off Erris Street), Cromwell 9310

Toilets flooded in history.

The Cromwell Historic Precinct is a unique visitor attraction dubbed 'Central Otago's best-kept secret'.[6] When the hydro dam at Clyde was completed in 1990, the beautiful Lake Dunstan was created, but Cromwell's main street disappeared under it. Wanting to preserve the area's heritage, a group of local residents had some of the historic buildings, dating back to the 1860s gold rush, saved or lovingly restored on higher ground that now forms the shores of Lake Dunstan. The resulting heritage precinct allows you to step back in time, exploring the area that comprises museum-style buildings, galleries, cafés and boutique shops. During spring and summer months, you can also enjoy the excellent range of local produce available from the Sunday Farmers and Craft Market.

Designed to be in keeping with the rest of the precinct, the Central Otago District Council installed a toilet block resembling an old shed. The facility was designed by designer John Meek and landscape architect Terry Emmitt who made use of corrugated iron veneer and stone steps to blend it seamlessly with the scenery.

...a group of local residents had some of the historic buildings, dating back to the 1860s gold rush, saved or lovingly restored on higher ground that now forms the shores of Lake Dunstan.

57

QUEENSTOWN PUB-CRAWL TOILETS

Pub on a Wharf (88 Beach Street), Muskets and Moonshine (10 Brecon Street), Jervois Steakhouse (8 Duke Street), & Cowboys (7 Searle Lane), Queenstown 9300

A Queenstown pub-crawl for your wee man!

Set on the shores of crystal clear Lake Wakatipu, and framed by majestic mountains, Queenstown's natural beauty and unique vibe provide a wonderful backdrop for holidays. The area is also considered the nation's adventure capital, offering a myriad of activities and experiences to satisfy the most hardened of adrenalin junkies.

Such appeal has skyrocketed the town's popularity, and there is now an endless list of bars and restaurants to choose from. If you're struggling to decide on which

ones to visit, why not let the urge to relieve yourself dictate a bar crawl through the town? Queenstown has four bars with toilets that are more entertaining-rooms than restrooms! Annoyingly for women, these toilets only tickle men's fancies while ladies' loos are a little lacklustre.

For men, visiting the conveniences can be so inconvenient when they have to miss out on the sporting action! Pub on a Wharf has the solution with a screen provided above the urinals!

It can also be just so darned dull for the dudes going to the dunny! So, for more amusement while they empty their bladders, Muskets and Moonshine bar has video game urinals controlled by the flow and direction of urine from their personal joystick.

And if guys are wondering how their, er ... joysticks measure up while at the Jervois Steak House, they should pay a visit to the urinals (provided by Queenstown Sofitel Body Corporate to service the building). An imposing photographic mural above the urinals features some intimidating images of women inspecting visitors' manhoods while they wee.

And finally, for a pee with a peevish purpose, Cowboys bar gives guys their pick of two heads to wet. Men can take aim and fire at busts of President Donald Trump or Welsh rugby writer Stephen Jones, which are placed in the urinals. Cowboy's previous bust of English referee Wayne Barnes came to an unfortunate end when his arm was somehow broken off. Don't ask!

An imposing photographic mural above the urinals features some intimidating images of women inspecting visitors' manhoods while they wee.

58

OAST HOUSE, CREEKSYDE HOLIDAY PARK

54 Robins Rd, Queenstown, Otago 9300

Did I come in to get p*ssed or to take one?

The Oast House toilets can be found within the Creeksyde Queenstown Holiday Park & Motels, an award-winning boutique holiday park in the centre of Queenstown. Just 5 minutes' walk from the bustling town centre, Creeksyde is nestled among 3.5 acres of beautifully landscaped gardens. Creeksyde has a very strong environmental ethos, which has been recognised with certification by Green Globe and EarthCheck, programs that provide global certification for sustainable tourism.

Creeksyde is well known for its out-of-the-ordinary design features and quirky

art. Examples include BBQ areas built from old plumbing fittings and flax thatched roofs, a sculptured 'tree' made from springs, saws and valves, and the Oast House bathrooms.

Oast House was built in 2009 and is modelled after old hop-drying buildings from the English brewing industry. The ladies' depicts a rainforest spa, while the men's looks like the inside of a pub. Vinyl prints on the walls are complemented by outstanding trompe-l'oeil (deceive the eye) floor paintings. The optical illusion may have men taking care not to fall down into the pub cellar and leave them confused as to whether they came in to get pi*sed or to take a p*ss! Rotorua artist, Mark Spijkerbosch, nephew of the owners of Creeksyde, Tonnie and Erna Spijkerbosch, did the paintings.

The ladies' depicts a rainforest spa, while the men's looks like the inside of a pub. Vinyl prints on the walls are complemented by outstanding trompe-l'oeil (deceive the eye) floor paintings.

59

ROXBURGH PUBLIC TOILETS

100 Scotland Street, Roxburgh, Otago 9500

*Perch yourself on these perfectly
polished pioneering privies!*

Unveiled in 2013, Roxburgh's ultra-modern facilities are fronted by a stunning, stainless steel sculpture of life-size figures on one side and an attractive vertical garden on the other. After consultations with the town's toilet beautification group, local sculptors Bill and Michelle Clarke incorporated the area's pioneering past into the design. Gold miners ventured into the area in the 1860s and began dredging along the Clutha River, and around a similar time, Roxburgh's thriving fruit industry began. Taking the sculptors 630 hours to create, the piece of art beautifully pays tribute to the Teviot Valley's fruit growing and gold mining history.

Bill and Michelle work from their private studio in Roxburgh, Forged and Crafted, and some of their other stainless steel masterpieces – a hare sculpture in the local park and a stainless steel sphere, illuminated at night – can also be seen around the town.

60

NORTH MAVORA LAKE DOC TOILET

Mavora Lakes Road, (Off SH 94), Mavora, Southland 9672

Lord of the Toilet Rings ... this toilet is 'my precious!'[7]

Spectacular this toilet is not, but the view from it is nothing short of stunning! Sitting in the middle of a Department of Conservation campground, this long drop loo may well be the most basic bog to feature in the guide. However, it is not the facility itself but the location that earns it a place on this 'must-do loos' list. Well and truly off the beaten track, you'll be rewarded for your efforts driving along the 39-km, no-exit, dusty, unsealed gravel road that brings you to North Mavora Lake. Peter Jackson must have considered this a special place too, choosing this area as the location for many scenes in the first Lord of the Rings film, The Fellowship of the Ring. The vast camping area enables campers to be virtually neighbour-free on their patch of earth, with camping fees that that certainly do not cost the earth. Such seclusion also means that if you're brave enough, you can actually leave the door open and take in the view from this loo! Try it, and you may find it is almost impossible to prevent the theme tune from spontaneously humming in your head as you admire the lake and mountainous backdrop. Don't tell too many people about this place; in the words of Gandalf the Grey: 'Keep it secret, keep it safe!'[8]

61

BILL RICHARDSON TRANSPORT WORLD AND CLASSIC MOTORCYCLE MECCA

491 & 25 Tay St, Hawthorndale, Invercargill 9810

Take a pit stop in a transport-themed loo-topia!

Bill Richardson Transport World and Classic Motorcycle Mecca may be world famous in New Zealand for its world-class collection of vehicles, but it also unexpectedly houses the country's most impressive range of novelty toilets in differently themed bathrooms. While the museum is bound to delight car, motorcycle and truck enthusiasts, the sheer size of the 15,000-sqm sheds and scale of the massive collection of 300-plus lovingly restored vehicles, set on two sites (Bill Richardson Transport World and Classic Motorcycle Mecca), is guaranteed to impress even the least petrol-headed among us. Parts of the museum transport you back in time and you can reminisce about old times (or imagine how life would have been back in the mid-1900s – depending on how old you are!) while walking along a street of old shop frontages or sitting in a retro cinema.

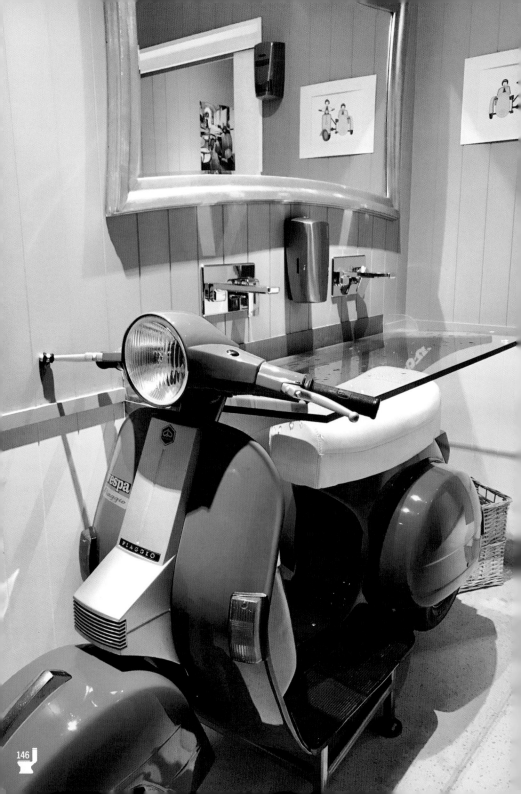

Appropriately, many of the bathrooms are in keeping with the transport theme. If something can be created from upcycled car parts, you'll find it here. Petrol pump basins, oil-barrel sinks, wheel-rimmed mirrors, toolbox vanities, toilet signs crafted from wheel nuts, racing car bucket seat toilet seats, and door handles fashioned from spanners, motorbike chains and petrol pump nozzles. And a ladies' powder room furnished with nothing less than a Vespa-supported vanity. Some restrooms have a more restful feel with their vintage design and sanitary features of a bygone era. Another bathroom will appeal to younger visitors – mirroring the huge lego-filled children's play area within the museum, it is vividly painted with lego-brick-styled basins. If you just want a bite to eat, you can appreciate two of these quirky bathrooms without entering the museums, as they are situated within the fabulous onsite cafés – The Grille at Bill Richardson Transport World and Meccaspresso at Classic Motorcycle Mecca. Both eateries offer a feast for your eyes as well as your taste buds with collections of transport-related artefacts and memorabilia.

DIG THIS INVERCARGILL
84 Otepuni Ave, Newfield, Invercargill 9810

Dunnies worth getting dirty for!

Dig This Invercargill is Transport World and Classic Motorcycle Mecca's newest attraction and New Zealand's first and only heavy equipment playground. This ground-breaking experience gives visitors the opportunity to operate bulldozers, excavators and skid steers in a giant gravel pit, and has received nothing but rave reviews since opening in 2017. There is even a mini-dig experience allowing guests as young as four years old to give it a go.

Building on the success of the loo-topia at Bill Richardson Transport World and Classic Motorcycle Mecca, director Joc O'Donnell put her creative hard hat on and designed construction-themed toilets – and guests definitely dig them! Door signs clearly indicate male and female toilets with their high-vis-jacket-wearing figures and comical warnings that they 'May contain traces of nuts' (the men's) or are a 'Nut-free zone' (the ladies')! Yellow and black striped barricade tape is a key design element in both of these pit stops and lighting is softened via yellow hard-hat lightshades. Repurposing a digger bucket as a wash station playfully brings a huge photograph of a digger into 3D reality. The toilets at Dig This Invercargill are certainly a ton of fun.

Earth Smart ®

Getting recycling on a roll...

12 rolls

Earth Smart®
recycled

100% recycled paper
Choose to be EarthSmart

BE EARTHSMART & RECYCLE YOUR SOFT PLASTICS

2 PLY 200 SHEETS 10 x 11cm

100% recycled paper,
100% recycled core,
recyclable packaging…

BE EARTHSMART
& RECYCLE YOUR
SOFT PLASTICS

Smart for you, Smart for the plane

www.earthsmart.co.nz

Bigger
& Softer*

Bigger & Softer*

Cotton Softs® **XL**

6 ROLLS 2 PLY

SUSTAINABLY SOURCED

RECYCLE SOFT PLASTICS

6XL = 13 STANDARD LENGTH ROLLS

softness & strength you can trust!

softness & strength
you can **trust!**

REFERENCES

1. Shane Walker, Email message to author, March 1, 2018.

2. Fork and Brewer (n.d.). Retrieved from www.forkandbrewer.co.nz

3. Mussel Inn (n.d.). Retrieved from www.musselinn.co.nz/About/about.html

4. Ministry of Education (n.d.) The Tremendous Tatty Patchwork Competition. Retrieved from http://shapingeducation.govt.nz/wp-content/uploads/2014/02/CERA-TATTY-ENTRY-FORM-AW.pdf

5. Wunderbar (n.d.). Elusive Toilets. Retrieved from www.wunderbar.co.nz/toilets.html

6. Cromwell Heritage Precinct (2018). Retrieved from www.cromwellheritageprecinct.co.nz/

7. Tolkien, J.R.R. (1973). The Hobbit. Boston, MA, United States: Houghton Mifflin Co.

8. Tolkien, J.R.R. (1988). The Fellowship of the Ring: Being the First Part of the Lord of the Rings (2nd Rep Edition). Boston, MA, United States: Houghton Mifflin Co.

PHOTOGRAPH CREDITS

All photos the author's own with the exception of:

Preface (p.5): ©Photograph (top left) by Puzzling World

Preface (p.5): Photograph (bottom right) supplied by Auckland Council

Waipu Cove Public Toilets (p.22/23): ©Daniel Mills

Camp Waipu Cove (p.24): ©Daniel Mills

Hot Water Beach Public Toilets (p.46, 47): ©Photographs by Brennan Thomas, supplied by Permaloo

Hahei Holiday Resort (p.48, 49): ©Grant Kilby, Hahei Holiday Resort

Waihi Surf Club Toilets: (p.52, 53): ©Photographs by Brennan Thomas, supplied by Permaloo

Diggelmann Park Public Toilets (p.54/55): ©Photograph by Brennan Thomas, supplied by Permaloo

Outhouse Public Toilets (p.58, 59): ©Photographs by Brennan Thomas, supplied by Permaloo

The Redwoods Shroud Art Toilets (p.60): ©Graeme Murray

The Redwoods Shroud Art Toilets (p. 61, 62/63): ©ROANZ Ltd

Benneydale Public Toilets (p.70/71): ©Photograph by Brennan Thomas, supplied by Permaloo

Hipapatua/Reid's Farm Recreation Reserve (p.72/73): ©Photograph by Brennan Thomas, supplied by Permaloo

Taupo Central Public Toilets (p.74): ©Gary Bennett

Emporium Eatery and Bar (p.75, 77): ©Photographs by Art Deco Masonic

Bay Skate (p.78/79): ©Bay Skate

Clifton Road Reserve Public Toilets (p.80/81): ©Simon Cartwright

Jailhouse Public Toilet (p.82, 83): ©OngaOnga Historical Society

Fork and Brewer (p.96): ©Photograph 1 by Russell Kleyn, supplied by Fork & Brewer

Mussel Inn (p.100, 101): ©Andrew Dixon, Mussel Inn

Takaka Public Toilets (p.103): ©Photograph by Elspeth Collier, supplied by Arthouse Architects Ltd

Mt Hutt Ski Area (p.120, 121): ©Photographs by Greg Young, supplied by Mt Hutt Ski Area

Puzzling World (p.128): ©Photograph by Puzzling World

Cromwell Town Centre Public Toilet and Bus Shelter (p.130/131): ©Photographs by Julian Apse, supplied by Mary Jowett Architects Ltd

Creeksyde Holiday Park (p.138, 139): ©Creeksyde Holiday Park

Bill Richardson Transport World (p.144, 145, 147): ©Olivia Turner (Image Photography and Design), supplied by Bill Richardson Transport World

Dig This Invercargill (p.148, 149): ©Olivia Turner (Image Photography and Design), supplied by Bill Richardson Transport World

Text and cover designed by Kuljit Kaur for BookPrint.

Edited by Marja Stack, Clearlingo

Produced by BookPrint Ltd.

First Printing, 2018

ISBN 978-0-473-44947-6

www.KiwiAsToilets.co.nz

MY FAVE LOO MEMORIES IN NEW ZEALAND